395

$5.00

JESUS AND THE AMERICAN MIND

HALFORD E. LUCCOCK
Professor of Homiletics, Yale University
Divinity School

THE ABINGDON PRESS
NEW YORK   CINCINNATI   CHICAGO

Printed in the United States of America

To
HENRY HALLAM TWEEDY

CONTENTS

FOREWORD

APPROXIMATELY half of the material in this volume was delivered as the Merrick Lectures of 1930 at Ohio Wesleyan University. The additional material has been added in the hope that the discussion of the themes might be somewhat less inadequate.

To President Edmund D. Soper, of Ohio Wesleyan University, I am deeply indebted for innumerable courtesies and kindnesses both before and during the delivery of the lectures.

HALFORD E. LUCCOCK.

CHAPTER I

OUR NATIONAL PORTRAIT

TOWARD the close of his book, *The America of To-day*, Mr. J. A. Spender asks this question, "How much of the Christian ethic can be absorbed into the immensely energetic, acquisitive, mundane life of a very prosperous people? Can the Kingdom which is not of this world hold its own in the actual world of wealth and power?" Mr. Spender does not attempt to answer the question. There is no answer. Time alone will bring one. But to get the question clearly before the mind, to see all that it involves, to look at it without the fog of facile optimism or merely conventional belief, is to take the first step toward framing an answer.

That question of the relation of the Christian ethic to the intricate complex of forces, qualities, and trends which make up American life finds a vivid symbol in the Detroit Art Gallery. Embedded in the wall of one of the rooms is a bit of mosaic of the second or third century, taken from the catacombs of Rome. It is a small section of a larger mosaic, but in it is worked out the Christian symbol of the fish. That crude and rough figure of a fish is a mute reminder of the grim but glorious day when to be a Christian was so dangerous that the name of Jesus must be represented by a secret symbol, the Greek word for fish—*ichthus*—representing the letters of the phrase, "Jesus Christ, Son of God, Saviour."

It is a long lane from the catacombs of Rome to the smokestacks of Detroit. There the mosaic looks out from the wall, a stirring relic of the first fine, careless rapture of Christianity, a symbol of an uncompromising religion and ethic, unafraid of the bright face of danger, now set down in the midst of the mother city of American industrialism. Is it any wonder that it seems out of place? Can the view of life which it symbolizes, the undiluted ethic of Jesus, the implications of its religious faith, ever be anything else but out of place in the Holy City of Mass Production and in the America of which that city is the consummate expression? Will the Christian conception of life be in this industrial civilization just what that mosaic from the catacombs is, a relic, a picture on the wall, a thing for crowds to look at with veneration, but unrelated to the dominant processes and motives of current life?

That little mosaic down in the dark of the catacombs conveyed an unyielding challenge to the whole structure of the Roman Empire, with its pomp, its slaves, its blood and lust, its rule of iron. A genuine Christianity, of which it is the symbol, has just as unequivocal a challenge to many of the fundamental assumptions and motives of the civilization around it to-day, its smoke and dollars, its production belts, its tickers, its long lines of job hunters, its human junk piles. Can the mosaic dominate the smokestack?

These questions look out on the whole issue of the Christian gospel in the machine age in America to-day. This volume does not attempt to answer the question of "how much of the Christian ethic can be absorbed in this acquisitive world." It essays, rather, the more modest task of exploring somewhat a few of the materials for an answer as they are found in American life. In particular it is concerned with what may be called some leading characteristics of the American mind, if in so conglomerate a collection of individuals, who make up the population of the United States, there can be found enough common traits to justify Thomas Jefferson's phrase, "the American mind." It is, of course, a large question with a thousand pitfalls for anyone with a flair for dogmatism. One of the most interesting features of the large body of literature of the estimates of American character is the frequency with which diametrically opposite qualities are set forth as fundamental American traits. There is hardly to be found in the long catalogue of human values and defects, from strident voices to the love of God, a single one which someone has not discovered to be the peculiar mark of Americans. Such an exhibit counsels caution. All that we shall endeavor to do here is to consider some traits which by the largest obtainable estimate and testimony seem characteristic of the American people to an extensive degree; that is, qualities which can truly be regarded as American in the sense that they are not equally European or merely human. In addition to that, there are included in the understanding of the vague phrase, "the American mind," the forces which are playing upon the mind and character of the American people in greater degree than anywhere else in the world. How do these qualities and forces relate themselves to the Christian purpose and social ideal? Which of them are congenial to the Christian ethic? Which of them are antagonistic, and how deadly is the antagonism?

It is hoped that by honestly looking at these questions and attempting to find at least partial answers to them, some light will be thrown on the dimensions and nature of the Christian task in America to-day. Multitudes within the church have never critically scrutinized from the Christian point of view the dominant forces and trends which are forming their minds. For that reason they have been attempting to build the kingdom of God with forces which are thoroughly antagonistic to it; or, to use a figure of speech with some authority, they have been attempting to harvest figs from thistles. The capital blunder of military strategy, that of mistaking foes for friends, has been and is being endlessly repeated.

It is doubtful whether one who does not feel a kind of baffling incongruity between the two can ever visualize with real understanding the problem of bringing together the mind of Jesus and the present mind of America. It is no wonder that there are multitudes to whom the figure of Jesus, brought into the modern scene, is like the advent of Rip Van Winkle. The clothes, the speech, the very ideas, proclaim him an enigma, wandering down from some remote height, hopelessly and pathetically out of date. He is greeted with the spirit if not the very words of the demons of Capernaum, "What have we to do with thee, Jesus, thou Nazarene? Art thou come to destroy us?" There is a tremendous incongruity, before which we may well pause in wonder, in the idea of Jesus of Nazareth being the proclaimed Master of the opulent, aggressive America of to-day. If we have never felt deeply that chasm, it simply means that we have a very partial and superficial understanding either of Jesus or of the real nature of our world. Maude Royden has very graphically expressed the amazement which there is in the fact that Jesus was ever accepted by Europe as its acknowledged Lord. She says:

And yet Europe received Christ. Oh, amazing conquest! Surely, the world has not yet realized the significance of the triumph. That China should hear Confucius, that India should receive the Buddha—these were easy conquests compared with the fact that Europe worships Jesus of Nazareth. What a God for a Charlemagne, a Hildebrand, an Otto! What a God for Europe! It does, I think, measure something of the power of Jesus Christ that this materialistic, egotistic Western world should be the place where his throne has been set.

If we say, "What a God for Europe!" may we not with equal wonder exclaim, "What a God for America!" The Jesus of the Galilæan roadside, the Jesus of the Sermon on the Mount, with his gospel of repentance, meekness, humility, and love, the God of the richest nation in the world—self-confident, self-assertive, energetic, acquisitive, industrial America!

Surely, as in the case of Europe, that very incongruity measures something of the power of Jesus. But it also gives a startling measure of the dimensions of the Christian task. Leaving aside entirely for the present the question of what is involved in making that formal acknowledgment of Jesus actual, the vivid recognition of contrast between Jesus and many of our most characteristic moods and tempers will do much to free us from the blindness of easy optimism, sentimentalism and complacency, the sins that do so easily beset a Christian church.   It will also help to make clear and urgent the necessity of validating the claim of Jesus to dominate the life of this changed world, not through any traditional authority, but as the sure way into the realization of life's highest values.

An inquiry into the characteristics of the mind of America, and into the action of the forces which are molding it at present, is timely for many reasons.

One reason is the prevalence of the mood of critical examination, now so largely evidenced in our literature and life.   Into what Matthew Arnold called, some fifty years ago, "the American rhapsody of self-praise" there have come many shrill discordant notes.   Indeed, in a very vocal element of the American family the pendulum has swung far to the other extreme.   Max Beerbohm has a striking pair of twin cartoons entitled the Nineteenth and the Twentieth Century.   In the cartoon depicting the Nineteenth Century we behold John Bull, a corpulent figure, full-fed on Jeremy Bentham, admiringly contemplating his figure in a mirror.   In the one for the Twentieth Century we see a long, sallow wisp of a young man, with a slim curved figure, gazing into a mirror.   But nothing is reflected back from the glass except a dim and shadowy question mark!   It is a fair picture of the questionings of the twentieth century in America.   If the mood cannot exactly be called humility, it is at least variously compounded of disillusionment, the puncture of complacency, and realistic thinking, frequently with a dash of cynicism.

For twenty years in increasing degree we have had a growing literature of self-criticism and self-condemnation, a visible and audible sign of a new mood. It reaches all the way from a serious evaluation of life to a raucous chorus of condemnation. We have grown heretical on the dogma that the evolutionary process ended in us as its crowning masterpiece. In Donald Ogden Stewart's *Aunt Polly's Story of Mankind* that amiable lady looked upon the process of evolution as the ascent from the nasty amoeba to Uncle Frederick standing radiant at the top of a long spiral slope, clothed in a Prince Albert, with one gloved hand resting on the First National Bank and the other upon the Presbyterian church. We are becoming fairly well reconciled to evolution; but we are beginning to have our doubts about Uncle Frederick! For a large number of Americans the calm peace of the days when they could repose in the sweetly solemn thought that they were the noblest work of God has been broken up. Principal L. P. Jacks went back to Europe after a trip in the United States, saying, "There is an element of misgiving like that of one who is traveling at a break-neck speed or standing on a giddy height. The voice of the pessimist is heard in the land." It is abundantly evident to eye and ear that American life does not seem to be satisfactory to a large number of inhabitants. A whole school of novelists is accurately named the "futilitarians." The true bill brought in contains a wide variety of discontents; American life is dull; it is ruled by plutocracy. Frightened native-born Americans proclaim it increasingly foreign and Jewish. Cynics roll the words "boob" and "moron" under

their tongues with a reiteration which becomes
slightly less exciting after a million repetitions; we
are uncivilized and soulless. At least there is a
notiable halt in the Hallelujah Chorus of self-satis-
facton.

One of the most promising elements in the present-
day scene is that a large body of intelligent people
look on life without any comforting illusions. Sinclair Lewis is acting as reporter for another group
of not strikingly intelligent citizens in the words
which he puts into the mouth of his loquacious
hero, Lowell Schmaltz, in *The Man Who Knew
Coolidge:*

"I tell you, Walt, I'm kind of puzzled. Sometimes I
almost kind of wonder (though I wouldn't want to be
quoted) whether with all the great things we got in this
greatest nation in the world, with more autos and radios
and furnaces and suits of clothes and miles of cement
pavements and skyscrapers than the rest of the world
put together, and with more deep learning—hundreds of
thousands of students studying Latin and bookkeeping
and doctoring and domestic science and literature and
banking and window-dressing—even with all of this, I
wonder if we don't lack something in American life."

In large measure this mood is a distinct asset.
The very vigor of self-condemnation makes for encouragement. There is more hope of moral growth
when one sighs than when one exults. "The end
of complacency," says Karl Barth, "may be the
first step back to faith." At least it may be the
first step toward a revaluation of the motives and
results of our present order of life.

A second reason for the timeliness of scrutinizing
from the standpoint of the ethics of Jesus the

forces which are making American life is the emergence of industrial and business processes which are
bringing revolutionary changes. Science and the
machine have combined to make a second industrial
revolution of more far-reaching consequences than
the first. A whole civilization is being destroyed
and a new one being set up. In the present generation scientific management and the methods of mass
production, mass consumption and stimulation, the
policy of low prices and high wages, are making a
more revolutionary age than that of Martin Luther.
It is these changes which led President Hoover to
declare that American capitalism of to-day is a
new and distinct thing in the world. André Siegfried, in a public lecture on his visit to the United
States in 1929, declared that his sense of separation from Europe felt here in America was in great
contrast to the feeling of nearness on his visit
thirty years ago. The distance, he said, is less;
the difference is greater. Then he felt at home; to-
day he feels a foreigner. That difference he ascribes
to present industrial and commercial processes. As
these new forces alter life for good or ill, it is a good
time to judge them from the large point of view
of essential human welfare. What are they doing
to life itself? Can they be made friend and ally,
or are they the irreconcilable foe of the Christian
ethic?

It is from the angle of Europe, however, that the
most acute questionings and fears concerning what
is called "Americanism" arise. To many on our
shores the Americanization of the world is the con-
summation devoutly to be wished. To many
Europeans it is a monster of hideous mien. Ramsay

Muir has put the feeling of Europe to-day into a vivid parody:

> "America the Golden,
>   With milk and honey blessed,
>   Beneath thy contemplation
>   Sink heart and voice oppressed."

There is a fear of American methods, not merely the advertising and hustle, but of the whole process, the numerical and machine-made standards, the materialism which threatens to break up the whole pattern of life and, to use a terrible verb, "Detroitize" the world.

One German economist says that this industrial and commercial system called "Americanization" is the strongest "apostolic and missionary force in the world." He finds that in spite of its horror it is making an irresistible appeal to the masses of Europe by its sanitation, its comforts, and its amusements. This fear of American standards and processes is not confined to Europe. It has become very vocal in Japan, for instance. A prominent writer of Japan, Takanobu Murobuse, in 1929 voiced this fear in a widely read lament that Japan, like the rest of civilization, has fallen under the domination of American gold, power, and ideas:

We all admit that the American dollar is the most powerful factor in the modern world, but there are many who do not realize that America, master of the gold and power, is also making the world's ideas. These people still cherish the illusion that Europe is the center of art, civilization, and culture. But look around you. What of our present-day life in Japan—is it not American rather than European? What is the Marunouchi Building (Tokio's greatest modern office building)?

What are these sports, this modern journalism, motor cars, jazz, radio, literature, all these ideas about rights of women, the spread of irreligion, the decline of philosophy, the mania for gold? All these we have taken from America. American ideas control the world in all phases of civilization. Europe still holds American culture in contempt, and most Japanese ape Europe in this respect, without realizing that we are all America's slaves materially and intellectually.

Deeper still, to Europe, the portent means not only American methods, but American control. On this Paul Hutchinson says:

The American economic threat is seldom absent from the mind of the European business man. In an article in the Neue Zuricher Zeitung last May, Edouard Herriot, leader of the French radicals, after prophesying the coming of some sort of European federation, exclaimed, "We must choose between European solidarity and American vassalism." This belief that European business is in danger of being swallowed wholesale is characteristic of large sections of Continental thought. To an American it does not seem to be a well-founded fear. But this does not change the fact that it exists everywhere in Europe, and has just as much influence as though it were well founded.

The greater part of Europe must work for generations to pay what are, ultimately, American claims. But the tariff policy of the United States puts that country in the position of refusing to accept the goods which represent the only commodity in which the European nations can pay. The United States thus has more exports than imports, and at the same time demands large cash payments in respect of debts. The only possible outcome, says the European, is an increase of the American capital investment, in one form or another, in other countries. In other words, Uncle Sam will establish a financial stake that may finally amount to economic control in European countries. And that, in the new era of world relations, will be practically equivalent to political domination.

Our present rate of investment in foreign countries is making for the overlordship of America—a prospect that would be irritating enough, even if the debt settlement were not working in the same direction. This mood of fear and irritation has not been notably allayed by the solemn moral lectures which Europe received gratis from President Coolidge. It is no wonder that a European conception of the United States has been expressed as "little Jack Horner enlightening the world." In 1928 the net increase of American long-term investments abroad was $1,339,000,000. It is not strange that much of Europe says,

> "My soul from out that shadow . . .
> Shall be lifted—nevermore.

This invasion is the A. E. F. translated into dollars —a war with silver bullets. We are seeing a curious parallel to some of the darker periods of European history. In the carnage known as the War of the Spanish Succession foreign nations fought out their battles in Germany and the surrounding states, using hired mercenaries in their armies. The same war for an imperial succession is now going on with different contenders. American automobile kings are carrying their battles into Europe, just as Marlborough and William of Orange used to carry their battles into Germany and Austria. Our American kings are likewise using French and German mercenaries in the fray. The end threatens to be a group of American economic colonies in Europe. It is small wonder that this prospect has been making for the social unification of Europe—all of which calls for a look at this imperialistic force called "Americanization." What is it in terms of ethical standards of life? What does it mean to the world?

Let us, then, step into the photograph gallery and try to get an idea of our own likeness. Our sharply defined viewpoint should be kept in mind that we are not merely exploring general characteristics but are trying to estimate them according to their harmony with or opposition to the Christian ethical ideal. This will mean endeavoring to rethink some of the ethical implications of the Christian faith in the modern world.

America has had her portrait taken more times than a débutante. This is fitting, for she is the world's première débutante, the first one, in fact, to come of age since the modern camera has been invented. In other words, as Bernard Fay observes, the United States is the first nation to be evolved since the process could be watched and measured by the new technique of the social sciences. For our photograph we cannot, of course, depend much on proclaimed and acknowledged ideals. If we went merely to ideals for our picture, then the American would emerge as Sir Galahad in a sack suit, or he would be, to change the haloes a bit, Saint George eternally fighting the dragons of a wicked world.

At the outset it is clear that if we are to get any realistic view of American character, we must work our way through a number of myths. Holy legends obscure the facts of American character; unholy legends as well. There are at least three well-defined clusters of tradition which obscure the view.

One is the classic view of the moral stature of Americans. It is patterned after the miracle of Cana in Galilee: God in his infinite wisdom reserved the best wine to the last. It is the staple of old-fashioned Fourth-of-July oratory, but it still thrives under the protecting shade of many resolute patriotic associations which keep alive the reverent practice of genuflexion to the sacred icon of American perfection. This view may well be called the "When-freedom-from-her-mountain-height" school of interpretation:

> "When Freedom from her mountain height
> Unfurled her standard in the air,
> She tore the azure robe of night
> And set the stars of glory there."

"The azure robe of night" has been torn to ribbons by a thousand orators and writers. Let two examples suffice. The first is Albert J. Beveridge, in a speech delivered in Indianapolis in that year of Manifest Destiny, 1898:

Fellow Americans, we are God's chosen people. Yonder at Bunker Hill and Yorktown his providence was above us. At New Orleans and on ensanguined seas his hand sustained us. Abraham Lincoln was his minister, and his was the altar of freedom the boys in blue set on a hundred battlefields. His power directed Dewey in the East, and delivered the Spanish fleet into our hands on liberty's natal day, as he delivered the elder Armada into the hands of our English sires two centuries ago. His great purposes are revealed in the progress of the flag, which surpasses the intentions of congresses and cabinets, and

leads us like a holier pillar of cloud by day and pillar of
fire by night into situations unforeseen by finite wisdom,
and duties unexpected by the unprophetic heart of selfishness. We cannot fly from our world duties; it is ours to
execute the purpose of a fate that has driven us to be
greater than our small intentions. We cannot retreat
from any soil where Providence has unfurled our banner;
it is ours to save that soil for liberty and civilization.
For liberty and civilization and God's promise fulfilled,
the flag must henceforth be the symbol and the sign to
all mankind—the flag!

But lest we think we have entirely outgrown that
self-portrait, look at a more recent example. It is
the editor of the Ladies' Home Journal who thus
delivers himself in the August, 1923, number:

There is only one first-class civilization in the world
to-day—it is right here, in the United States. It may
be a cocky thing to say, but relatively it is first class,
while Europe is second class, and Asia fourth to sixth
class.

Amen! The trouble with the Narcissus school
is not that its practitioners do not have authentic
material to work on; it is, rather, that the haloes
block the camera.

Equally distorted is the classic European picture
which has been done over with a thousand variations
on the same theme—the American shown full
length as the materialistic dollar chaser, thrown
into startling relief when placed beside the serene
idealism of Europe. No matter how strict the
immigration laws under the quota, no effective bar-
rier has been set against the flood of foreign labor
which comes in yearly under the classification
"lecturers" to give impassioned lectures on Ameri-

can materialism at five hundred dollars a lecture. This portrait is often drawn in a naïve assumption that material acquisitiveness is an American invention like the incandescent light, or a tree never indigenous to Europe, like that from which quinine is derived.   A whole train of far-sighted observers have supplied a corrective to this European mythology, beginning with de Tocqueville and extending down through Bryce, the noblest of them all, Münsterberg, Wells, Siegfried, Santayana, and others. But the cartoon as presented with the generous help given by a million American travelers in Europe prevails.   The common man in the streets of Europe sees across the water through a glass darkly.

A current freak mirror held up to America with the cordial invitation to behold herself is what might be called the American portrait, modern style.   The camera used by this impressionist group of photographers has all modern attachments—a cynical lens and a contemptuous finder.   We do not need to describe its technique or its major artists—they are ever with us.   With this school the American bird has undergone a transformation. It is no longer the spread-eagle; it has become the hoot-owl.   Now, of course, the owl has a reputation for wisdom, but it did not get it by hooting; it got it by keeping still.   There is no more wisdom in a hoot of disdain than there is in a scream of uncritical adulation.   These hooters in the forest have had their method well described by J. St. Loe Strachey, in his book, *American Soundings*.   Writing about H. L. Mencken he says that Mr. Mencken's technique consists of going out into the streets

and dragging in all the dead cats he can find into
the parlor and saying, "Here is America, look at it!"
There is no more curious or amusing type of book
than that being produced in some quantities in
Europe by authors who have engaged in researches
in the back numbers of the American Mercury,
supplemented by some earnest conversations with
American expatriates in the sidewalk cafés of Paris.
A schoolboy once described the well-known painting
of the Revolutionary War, "The Spirit of '76," by
saying that it was a picture of three men: "one of
them had a fife, one of them had a drum, and one of
them had a headache." This modern school of discontent has a headache as its principal item of critical apparatus. The result is that there is more
discomfort than insight. The present vogue of the
literature of detraction has created in front of
publishers' offices a large traffic jam of authors
anxious to cash in before the fashion changes.
Undoubtedly, the vogue is beginning to pall. Even
within the sacred covers of the American Mercury
the familiar slap-stick comedy begins to tire after
the thousandth repetition. Even among the en-
lightened there is a growing suspicion that the
American octave includes more than the one bass
note. Some are even remembering that while in
America there is the National Security League,
there is also the Civil Liberties Union. There is
not only William Jennings Bryan, but Justice Oliver
Wendell Holmes; not only Henry Ford, but Jane
Addams.

Getting safely past the stock caricatures, let us
turn to the rest of the family album, keeping clearly
in mind the purpose of our observation that we are

not attempting a psychoanalysis of the American
soul, not going on a sight-seeing tour or conducting
a statistical excavation.

Two points of difficulty confront any assay of
American character. One is the infinite variety of
Americans; the other is the variety of historical influences. From these come the baffling contradictions
present in our life. No wonder that Mr. Siegfried says,
"No other country is so difficult to understand or so
complex in its moral structure." For these reasons,
after the most exhaustive research and the most
unassailable analysis and cataloguing of American
traits, there should appear at the end of such a
research Mr. Dooley's famous "errata."   Mr.
Dooley says that in his early years he wrote a book
about women. Some years later, when he came to
republish it, after a critical reading he inserted in the
front this statement with the scientific name "Errata": "Wherever in this volume appears the word
is, substitute *is not*, and wherever the words *is not*
appear, substitute *may be*, *perhaps*, or *God knows*."
It is well to distrust any generalizations unaccom-
panied by such a saving footnote.

No continent presents a greater geographical
variety. The Everglades and the Rockies, the
marshes of New Jersey and the wheatfields of
Nebraska, the Maine woods and the deserts of
Arizona—all are America. In like manner no
continent stretches a wider range of character.
Most generalizations about America can be set
down as false, too easy, or too hurried. The population is too vast, too many-sided, the elements
too diverse to be caught in any single formula. No
one adjective can be stretched all the way from

Boston to Hollywood; it is bound to crack some-where along the three-thousand-mile trek.

Partly as a result of this variety we present the spectacle of a people of the most amazing and unbelievable contradictions. These contradictions are the key to the confusion in many books about America. For without knowing the historical reasons for the dominant traits in the people and the elements making up the population, one em-barks on a chaotic sea of mutually exclusive asser-tions. Take just a few of the more obvious as samples.

1. Few would withhold from the average American the adjective "practical." Practical-mindedness was a necessity to survival in a virgin forest and on a moving frontier. Yet this practical-minded people is also one of the most sentimental nations in the world; its sentimentalism has won for it a world-wide reputation for hypocrisy.

2. A primary trait of the American character, by common consent, is individualism. Yet what nation surpasses us for gregariousness? We have empha-sized the rights of the individual; yet we so cling to our kind that we have developed a sort of national *agaraphobia*, a fear of open places.

3. Ours is a business civilization; "the land of the dollar" is the usual appellation bestowed from abroad. We are dominated by profit making; yet, spending money with a free hand, we display amaz-ing generosity.

4. We have an astounding variety; yet we are marked by a similarity and monotony which has become a by-word among our critics.

5. As a young nation we have been marked by

an intense interest in the future. We have not been able to look back to a long past; both our past and present have been in the future! Yet along with this interest in the future we have displayed a carelessness about the future which few nations have approached.

6. America is radical in its business methods, that is, of course, within the general limits of the capitalistic system. At the same time we are extremely conservative in political thinking and action.

7. In our approach to many questions we display a hard-bitten realism. We are also marked in other aspects and often in the same fields by a genuine idealism.

This list of glaring contradictions might be far extended. Yet, with all these things in view, American mentality is a distinct thing in the world, not only by reason of historical causes, but also by the action of present forces. Siegfried speaks of our "completely original society." O'Higgins and Reed, in their book, *The American Mind in Action*, agree with Siegfried:

Perhaps there is no such thing as an American mind. Perhaps—in the sense of the humorist who complained that the country had weather but no climate—the variety among Americans is so great and the mass of the people so little homogeneous that no sort of common psychology can be rightly computed to them. Nevertheless, there are certain traits and mental qualities that are accepted as characteristically American; and when the critic of America assembles those traits and mental qualities together into a sort of synthetic man, he is commonly allowed to consider this creature of his selective fancy a typical American with a typical American mind.

Even where the problems in American civilization are the same as in Europe they are characterized here by an intensity which makes their effect on the people unique. The development of character and temperament has been quite like that of such inventions as the railroad system, for instance. In the early days of the railroad system European and American engineers were at work on its development at the same time. There was very little exchange of ideas. When the American system emerged in a developed form, it was quite different from that wrought out in Europe and a thoroughly peculiar American product.

For our portrait we depend not only on the features agreed upon by our own observers, but on the large collection of travelers' tales. Certainly, for a century and a half we have been cynosure of neighboring eyes. A vast literature has rolled up which is good for our humility of soul; and also much of it is a first aid to our sense of humor. These travelers have brought with them every variety of attitude: hate, malice, curiosity, desire to learn, gullibility, and even love.

Matthew Arnold said of Goethe that he put his finger on Europe and said, "Thou ailest *here*—and *here*." Our modern probers have far outdone the conservative Goethe. They have said, "Thou ailest here, and here, and here, and here . . ." even up to the Nth power. Surely, after such a regimen we are in the mood for the General Confession— "There is no health in us." These observers came for all reasons, to make money, to prove a theory, to interpret honestly. Frequently the amount of money depended on the unfavorableness of the report.

Sam Weller, Sr., traced this relation very frankly when he said, "And then let him come back and write a book about the 'mericans, as 'll pay his expenses and more if he blows 'em up enough."

Dickens himself followed this formula to vast financial profit. For a generation the literary tour in preparation for a book has become almost as standardized as an itinerary prepared by Messrs. Cook & Son to see Europe in thirty days for six hundred dollars, tips included. The great man lands in New York and interviews a few local celebrities and visits a dozen speakeasies to enable him to speak authoritatively on prohibition. At 12:45 P. M., he catches the Twentieth Century Limited to Chicago. Between the grapefruit and the egg at breakfast next morning he sums up the Middle West in an epigram while looking out of the dining-car window. In Chicago he writes down a few witticisms about machine guns, and, coming East again, catches the Mauretania on the return trip. Stuart Chase has outlined a popular variation of this standard tour: "One distinguished foreigner after another visits the assembly line of Mr. Ford and a Rotary Club at its luncheon ceremonies, and from thence departs on the next liner, impatient to put on a rotary press one more volume announcing that machines are reducing Americans to automata." In his indispensable book, *As Others See Us*, John Graham Brooks says that "there are at least twenty volumes by French travelers from which one could take away the various and picturesque titles reproducing them by 'A Whole Afternoon in the United States.' Of some of them one would have to say that the day was very ill spent." In this international sport, however, Germany has recently taken the palm from France. The world's champion for speed photography is Count Herman Keyserling. He openly boasts of the fact that he wrote his section on America in his *Travel Diary of a Philosopher* in two weeks. In his *America Set Free* he expresses the fear that by staying in this country several weeks he remained so long that the sharpness of his first impressions was dulled!

This reminds one of the comment of Philip Guedalla on Napoleon III: "The emperor had once stayed at the Washington Hotel on Broadway; and he suffered for twenty years from the hallucination that he understood America." We are tempted to think that among this crowd of travelers there had been a good many descendants of Sinbad the Sailor, with forefathers on the maternal side deriving from Baron Münchhausen. An added interest in these stories is the fact that we are abnormally sensitive to foreign opinion, a trait which the modern Freudian, of course, would have no trouble in setting down to the inferiority complex of a young country. A large majority of the comments made in the books of travelers published up to 1840 could be explained as the natural accompaniment of our period of development. The early criticisms were concerned largely with the inconveniences of a nation in the making; the bad roads, greasy food, the hotels, the boarding houses. Even the Jersey mosquitoes appeared in the international literature before 1830. The first place is nearly always occupied by three astounding novelties of America— ice water, rocking chairs, and ice cream. Niagara Falls was the only thing in America which all

travelers condescended to praise.   Most of the early
criticism from our 'English relatives is not better
than that of any other country.   It is savage and
contemptuous.   Summing it up, John Fiske said,
"One good thing, and one only, was admitted to have
come from America—quinine."   In contrast to this
stands the confession of De Tocqueville, a noble
word that might well serve as a motto for all travelers
everywhere, "I grant that in America I saw more
than there was to see."   For that reason De Tocqueville, looking through the eyes of faith and imagination, was almost alone among all the interpreters
in the first seventy-five years in seeing the potential
greatness of the nation.   Down to the present
day the commenters have noted down their judgments: we are too fat; too thin; too tall; too short;
we have no inner soul; no tranquillity; no moderation; no real culture; no prospective.   Or, to sum it
all up in a massive insight of Keyserling, we are just
animals.

Yet out of this, by the very reiteration from
travelers of the greatest difference of viewpoint
and nationality, there are a large number of common
estimates.   Let us take a deep breath, brace ourselves, and look at the picture which comes out
from these estimates of foreign observers and from
evaluations originating in America.   On one point
only there seems to be well-nigh universal agreement by foreigners.   All graciously admit our
national talent for bragging.   The evidence is too
much to be denied.   The quotation from Senator
Beveridge a few pages back was one out of thousands
of samples which could readily be supplied.   Such
native productions do more to establish our genius

for self-praise than any of the stinging travesties
of Dickens in his *American Notes* or *Martin Chuzzle-
wit*. This talent has been summed up by one
American as "congenital eminence." In the presence of such a talent the citizens of other nations
often felt in the mood of the Red King in *Alice in
Wonderland*. Irritated by Alice's amazing and sudden growth following the eatingof the magic biscuit,
the Red King promulgated Rule 42, "All persons
over a mile high must leave the court." Americans,
so the European theory went, being by their own
measurement over a mile high, were ruled out of
court.

After this first point of agreement we find the
following among the generally recognized lines of
the portrait:

Democracy
Energy
Initiative
Devotion to Equality
Liberty
Adventurousness
Youth
Good will
Kindness
Optimism
Individualism
Courage
Practicalness
Religious spirit
Self-reliance
Generosity
Adaptability
Complacency

Money domination
Hurry
Gregariousness
Sentimentalism
The "get ahead" spirit
Wastefulness
Parochialism
Externalism
A passion for organiza-
    tion
Supremacy of business
Lawlessness
Worship of size
Conformity
Standardization
Exaggeration
Superficiality

How delightful if we could wear the laurels and cast off the liabilities! But the very word "liability" leads us into the heart of the problem.

The chief liabilities of any people come not alone from their defects or deficiencies; they come, indeed, from their very virtues and strength. In American history there has been large scope for the operation of "the deadly virtues," that is, the perversion of good qualities or their unbalanced assertion and expression. We cannot divide the above qualities, or any list of qualities, into good and bad. The delusion that life could be arrayed in such naïve simplicity has betrayed the Christian Church into its present comparative impotence. The church has shown a capacity to recognize the traditional deadly sins. It has been largely blind to the equally deadly virtues. Consequently, it has given its benediction to forces and qualities which worked against its own purpose. Take optimism, for just one example. It is a great and noble quality of soul, true; at times it is the very stuff by which the kingdom of God is built. It shades over into a resolute faith which has subdued kingdoms, stopped the mouths of lions and put to flight armies of aliens. The church has persistently lauded the virtues of optimism and berated pessimism. It has been oblivious to the fact that a large amount of optimism is an unrivaled obstacle to the operation of Christian ideals in the world of business. "Optimism" as a part of the ritual of the worship of progress says, "Hush, hush" to every unpleasant and disturbing truth. It will tolerate almost any evil sooner than disturb the orderly march of business to a bigger balance. One of the most depressing things in

America to-day is the optimism of a typical business group. For such optimism means that everything is about all right, and that, of course, means that the present order of life is just about the best that we can hope for. Could there be a more serious antagonist to a Christian hope for a better world? So it is with nearly every other so-called good quality on the list. The question that needs to be raised about each trait is, upon what goal does it focus? What the Christian transformation of life needs is not so much a set of new qualities as new purposes for old forces.

This list of features of American mentality is arbitrarily selected for examination, yet it contains the qualities most generally noted and some which have found most frequent and evident expression historically. The inclusion of some of the above qualities will be regarded by some people as additional evidence of American egotism and boastfulness. The inclusion of others will be looked upon as a slander. Doubtless some characteristic American qualities have been left out. A list equally long might be added without exhausting the traits manifested by large numbers of Americans. Many forces have been left out, some of which will be discussed later.

But for the present they give the lines of a composite portrait. How does it fit into the mind of Jesus? How truly do they represent the majority of Americans? How many of these qualities are allies of the ethical and social ideal of Christianity? How many are there antagonistic to it? Has the church been like the man in Jesus' story in the gospel who waged war without seeing all which the campaign involved, or clearly understanding the nature and strength of the enemy? To these questions we now turn.

CHAPTER II

AMERICAN TRAITS
AND THE PURPOSE OF JESUS

THE very attempt to get the Christian ideal into definite, compact statement involves an impossibility. "Make any truth too definite," says Coleridge, "and you make it too small." The teaching of Jesus is like the tent in an old Oriental fairy story, which was made of material so delicate that it could be folded up and easily contained in the palm of a man's hand; yet when it was unrolled and set up it would afford shelter for an army of thousands of men. The very phrase, the Christian social ethic, seems to beg a large question, as though it were a definite pattern of some exact mechanical form which we could lay down and into which we could force life. Indeed, it is often assumed that Christian teaching is a bed of Procrustes. The effort to find the consequences of the teaching of Jesus for social life carries us over highly controversial ground, like the battlefield of Waterloo, over which armies have fought for centuries. Debates have been waged for centuries not only over what the Christian social ideal is, but over the previous question, Is there any? The inquiry carries us back into some major questions in the last fifty years of Christian thinking and into some highly debated issues of New Testament criticism of the present time. We have still with us the sharply individualistic interpretation of Christianity,

such as expressed in the following words of Dean
Inge:

The strength of Christianity is in transforming the
lives of individuals—of a small minority, certainly, as
Christ clearly predicted, but a large number in the ag-
gregate. To rescue a little flock, here and there, from
materialism, selfishness, and hatred is the task of the
Church of Christ in all ages alike, and there is no likeli-
hood that it will ever be otherwise.

When such an expression is put alongside of Dean
Inge's disdain for democracy and distrust of social
action, he seems like "the compleat Tory." But
these words are a fair summary of the position of
many and the unconscious and unexpressed assumptions of a multitude.

In consideration of the social implications of Jesus'
teaching the necessity for the utmost care and
honesty in dealing with the records must be stressed.
A constantly recurring feature of Christian history
has been a forcible capture of Jesus. The scene in
the Garden of Gethsemane, where he is overpowered
by the Roman soldiers and forced to go along with
them, has been repeated again and again. He has
been captured by the forces of the ecclesiasticism
and his words warped into the support of positions
which he assailed all his life. In a like manner he
has been captured for absolutist theories of political
power, for militarism, and materialistic economics.
Also he has been forcibly impressed into the support
of particular theories of social reform. In the cause
of thoroughgoing ethical and social reconstruction
of society men have dragged Jesus along with them.
They have read back into his teaching ideas quite

foreign to his time and to his own thought forms. Such excessive zeal is as mistaken as any other form of dishonesty.

In particular, we must be on our guard lest we press the phrase "the kingdom of God" into a meaning too forcibly harmonized with modern social conceptions. We must remain open-minded on the amount of apocalyptic teaching which that phrase had as it was used by Jesus. Whatever the apocalyptic element in that idea, the religious and ethical bases for a Christian social order do not depend on the precise meaning of that phrase as used by Jesus or as understood by his adherents. The Christian ethic for society has a broader basis in the whole personality and spirit of Jesus, in the implications of his faith in God, in the nature of the God in whom he believed, in his whole conception of life, its values and ends, and in his conception of man.

We must get rid, moreover, of the false antagonism still raised in many quarters between individual and social conceptions of Christianity. The attempt to draw a sharply divided line between a man's inner life and the external social order is false psychology as well as false religion. It is true, of course, as has been pointed out times without number, that certain aims we realize as individuals and certain others we realize only by acting together. But that does not mean that the whole external mechanism of life, its economic and industrial interests, property, the relation between races, are foreign to the life of the spirit. On the contrary, these things are inseparable parts of life of the spirit. Life is all of one piece. For centuries men have had a hopeless undertaking acting as though they could spiritualize the life of an individual, isolated as it were, in a vacuum, and leave the society which is made up of individuals in control of a ruthless and predatory selfishness which is in direct opposition to the spiritual forces supposedly in control of life. It is that kind of an impossible conception which has brought the world to its present plight.

Neither will we get a clear insight into Jesus' teaching if we do not realize that he was not primarily a social reformer or a social legislator. His teaching assuredly was to issue in a new society, but his primary purpose was not to make social changes. It was to make new men. His interest was focused on the making of a man whose social mind would be controlled by good will. But while he was not primarily a social reformer, it is clear that the purpose of God, as Jesus interpreted it, included all aspects of life. His ideal for man was a society in which men acknowledged their sonship to God and sought the common good of men as their brothers. Nor was Jesus a lawgiver. Had he been that, he would be to-day only a half-forgotten addition to the company of superseded legislators. Any code of laws he could have framed would have become obsolete with social changes; new forms of sin, particularly the baffling forms of corporate sin, which mark the modern age, would have been left wholly out of view. Instead of that inevitable obsoleteness Jesus remains a timeless Master of life whose principles have abiding validity and test any social order. It might be said that the lesson which Jesus gave to the world was not a lesson like one in geometry in which we have the definite answer to begin with; it was more like a lesson in algebra in which we are to work out the implications of the relations between certain given terms.

We have said that Jesus' ethical teaching springs from his religion; it is an implication of his idea of God, his faith in and experience of God. It is impossible to separate the religious and ethical teaching of Jesus. Like his personality, his teaching is a whole. In trying to separate the ethical teaching from the religious we lose both; each fades like a flower which withers when plucked. Jesus had absolute faith in the goodness of God. That was the first attitude which he strove to develop in his followers; it was the source of his whole conception of man and of life. From that faith in a living God there came the content, the motive, and the dynamic of the good life. "Without this faith in God the ethics of Jesus would never have been taught."

From this faith, then, sprang his teaching. Let us try to put some of it in simplest form. The most obvious summary would be that Jesus' message for society is involved in his teaching of the Fatherhood of God and the brotherhood of men, But those phrases have become such a stereotype that, noble and essential as they are, they frequently obscure thinking like the descent of a Newfoundland fog. Indeed, much of the paralyzing generality of the witness of the church on industrial and economic questions comes from this thick fog. Nothing is more futile then the constant repetition of principles so general that they apply to nothing in particular and can always be evaded in a definite concrete situation. Thus many Christians have no trouble in accepting a formal belief in divine Fatherhood and human brotherhood, who are stirred to frenzy if some perfectly logical and inevitable deductions from those doctrines are made, exactly in the manner of those who used to rise and march out of church when the subject of slavery was introduced. The brotherhood of man was one thing; opposition to slavery was another.

Sacredness of personality is one center of Jesus' religious and ethical teaching. To Jesus men were children of God. That fundamental faith is accurately, as well as poetically, expressed in the unsystematic theology of the Negro spiritual, "All God's Chillun Got Wings." This is not a romantic assertion of human perfection, it is an unshakable faith in the divine worth and possibilities of human beings. Harnack says, "Jesus Christ was the first to bring the value of every human soul to light, and what he did no man can any more undo." That central teaching is the ultimate test of any civilization. Following out its implications would turn much of our present order upside down, for it means that human values must take precedence of all else in the world. A person is not a thing to be bought and sold, exploited and tossed aside like a squeezed orange. A man is never a tool or a hand; he is a spark of the Divine. We can gain no more clear or staggering picture of the Christian task in the United States to-day than to see that it is just to make that truth at home in Pittsburgh, Chicago, the coal fields of West Virginia and textile towns of North Carolina.

A corollary of the realization of the sacredness of

personality is the necessity of faith in man. That man is worthy of faith was an assumption on which Jesus habitually acted. Such basic faith also finds expression in another verse of that same Negro spiritual, "All God's Chillun got a robe." Throughout the New Testament the robe is the symbol of redemption. That old Negro song, the product of an authentic religious experience, proclaims the redeemability of human nature. It is a faith indispensable to the establishment of genuine brotherhood. Race prejudice, class discriminations, aggressive and suspicious nationalism, have all flourished because of the blighting skepticism concerning man.

The sacredness of personality implies the duty of society to the extent within its power, to provide opportunity for the highest possible realization of every personality. "I am come that they might have life and have it abundantly." If man is a spiritual being, he must not be denied opportunity for spiritual development. Hence, labor that stunts and degrades personality cannot be tolerated. "True democracy is the opportunity for man to grow spiritually tall." The materialism which sacrifices the realization of the personality of men, women, and children to the supposed necessities of industry or business is a deadly obstacle to the kingdom of God.

Basic in Jesus' view of life is the reality of human fellowship, the solidarity of mankind. With Jesus, anything which displaces brotherhood by antagonism is evil. Whatever denies fellowship, whatever limits it, be it selfishness, nationalism, race hatred, or autocratic domination, whether political or industrial, is evil; not to be tolerated in a Christian society. Co-operation rather than selfish competition is both the norm and the goal.

Love as the motive of life, with the consequent duty of service devolving on all, is a related center of Jesus' ethic. In this the root of the ethic in religion is clear. Jesus believed that love is possible and practicable as the mainspring of human relations, because God is love. When Jesus lifted up this motive of love from the area to which it was usually restricted, that of the family, he did four things: he deepened it till it got down to the inner motive; he heightened it till it reached up to the character of God; he extended it till it stretched across every fence and wall; he incarnated it in his whole life. If love means anything at all, it means the subordination of private gain to the spirit of service. It means a society free from covetousness, self-seeking willingness to take material profit at the expense of another person. Consequently, self-sacrifice is an inevitable necessity of love.

These truths are platitudes; that is both the hope and despair. It is the hope of a better order, in that the fact that they have become platitudes means a constantly spreading recognition of the disentangled Jesus, separated from all the accretions which during the centuries have disguised and distorted his real nature and purpose. It is a despair, for it means that they have become for many merely blunted and dead truths. They have become bedridden truths which never walk among men. They are like dynamite carried in cases so strong that there is no danger of their exploding. If these truths are taken seriously and not with stultifying sentimentalism, they will project who ever so takes them into a conflict. Yet these truths must be used or lost. Religion must function in the social world or be sloughed off. It will become like the appendix of the human body, something which once had a function, but is now at its best a useless vestige, and at its worst a dangerous point of infection. Religion, if it conduces to a facile and premature peace in its followers, a dimming of their conscience, is a dangerous moral infection.

Christianity cannot be shut up into a private chapel surrounded by a moat. Matthew Arnold said that conduct was three fourths of life. To-day economic activity is for multitudes of people nine tenths of life. Banishing God from this nine tenths of life makes him like some medieval prince who maintained a claim to a province which was acknowledged in only a few little villages here and there, and those not the most significant ones.

If we accept these truths, we are committed to quite distinct positions; for instance, that civilization is to be judged by the human balance sheet; not by the mountain of things produced, but what happens to the human agents in the process. We are bound to work for such a transformation of industrial organization as may make industry a fellowship in common service instead of a struggle for personal advantage.

What kind of soil does America furnish for this sort of an ethical ideal and goal? The word "soil" brings to mind that classic parable of Jesus born out of his own personal experience, the parable of the soils. The prospect of Jesus' message in America is portrayed by that parable in terms of our own day. Look at it literally in terms of geology for a moment. If we ask the question, What kind of a soil has America for any seed? the answer is: All the varieties known to nature, both favorable and hopeless. Trying to grow Christian fruits of character from certain strongly rooted American qualities is like trying to grow palm trees in the Adirondacks or Oregon apples in Death Valley. One does not need to be a cynic to say that for some peculiarly Christian qualities, such as humility, for instance, the dominant traits of America are emphatically a Death Valley.

Set the parable of the soils down in the United States—how closely it fits—like a glove! First, there is the hard-beaten roadway; a picture of the hard life where truth has no more chance to lodge and grow than a grain of seed would have on the concrete surface of the Lincoln Highway. What a hard soil the present widespread mood of complacency and self-satisfaction in the United States offers to the revolutionary ethics of Jesus, to his demand for repentance, to the forthright rebuke which his high estimate of human personality makes to much of our whole order of life!

Then there is the seed on the shallow soil, a true picture of the difficulty of getting superficial and unrealistic sentimentalism, which is so strong a mark of multitudes, including multitudes of Christians, to face and pay the cost of a sincere effort to apply Jesus' teaching.

Again, what a picture of America it is which Jesus draws of the crowded life—"some seeds fell among thorns and thorns sprang up and choked them." Choked—that is the proper word for the greatest profusion of material things ever assembled!

Preoccupied minds and hearts choked—strangled, by a huge accumulation of external things crowding out the life of the spirit, leaving little or no room for the purpose of Jesus to grow.

Is there no good soil? Only a perverse blindness could fail to see the application of the good soil in Jesus' parable to the American mind and character, temperament and traits. Some of our most evident characteristics are well fitted to bring the good seed of the Kingdom to a thirty, sixty, and hundredfold fruit. To recognize this is not by any means to fall into the complacency which we have likened to the hard, smooth pavement. Take one quality, for instance, emphasized by foreigners, as well as Americans, as one of our outstanding traits, helpfulness, good will. It is not by any means an exclusive American trait, but it is a persistent one of wide diffusion. Hugo Münsterberg links helpfulness with honesty as the "most essential characteristics of Americans." Helpfulness shows itself in charity, in hospitality, in projects for education or for public improvements, or in the most trivial service of the daily life. "If it were given to me," says Santayana, "to look into a man's heart and I did not find good will at the bottom, I should say without any hesitation, 'You are not an American.' " If the indictment of these foreign critics be true, what more promising soil could there be for some seeds of Jesus' message to bear fruit? It is one of the national characteristics which joins hands with the Christian ethic in the making of a Christian society. There are others which will be noted. With these our task is not to create a soil for the growth of the Christian ideal, but, rather, to ward off the forces which block the working out of this native endowment. Indeed, the observation just made may well apply to many of the qualities in the list set down a few pages back. Let us examine a few very swiftly.

First of all, let us hasten to say that many of the traits most universally called American are emphatically sixty and hundredfold soil for the seeds of the kingdom of God. We are tempted to say that there is nothing more needed at the present time in the United States than a strengthened appreciation of the spiritual and ethical resources of American character. The vociferous cynicism now finding expression, more interested in sprightly epigrams than in serious evaluations, the literature of the mud puddle, the painful straining for a showy sophistication, even, at times, also the deeply serious troubling of sensitive consciences over the evils of our national life, have all led to a widespread underestimate of the genuine Christian assets in American life. This has resulted at times in a kind of defeatism in the Christian forces which seems to picture the Christian ideal as pulling against the whole current of American life. Nothing will correct such a mood more than the critical recognition that there are many qualities which do fit the mind of Jesus as superb building material. Jesus is at home with many of our strongest traits and moods.

One of the world's greatest stories is that of *The Wandering Jew*. It is a story which symbolizes a profound truth of Christian history. The hero of this medieval tale is one who is supposed to be condemned by Jesus to immortality on earth. He can never retire completely from the human scene, but must reappear in each new generation as its contemporary. In a high and reverent sense Jesus is the Wandering Jew. He does not come upon the scene in each new century as a Rip Van Winkle, but as the contemporary of each new age, the one in whom its highest aspirations find fulfillment. When the age of democracy came on the world's calendar, it found in Jesus its highest exponent and leader. So it is with many other characteristic interests of our time. Most of our attention later in this book will be given to the obstacles and antagonistic forces which the teachings of Jesus meet in present American trends. Here is recorded an appreciation of the allied forces. It is just as poor strategy to underestimate allies as it is to underestimate enemies.

Let us glance at a few recognized qualities. First on almost every list of American traits would be democracy, a devotion to it and a faith in it; a devotion and faith, of course, more evident often than the practice of it, but nevertheless an ineradicable mark, a powerful ideal. Must our awareness of the difficulties of its application, its gross denials in industry and race relations, its corruption in politics, and our revulsion against much of the spacious propaganda use made of democracy during the Great War blind us to its essential harmony with the ideas of Jesus? The belief that the control of life should not be in the hands of the few but of the many closely fits Jesus' conviction of the reality of human brotherhood and the worth of the individual soul. It is an authentic expression of his evaluation of the common man. A faith in democracy is the driving force of many of the movements working toward a more ethical life. It finds expression in the historical American devotion to the benefits of culture for the whole people. It has been a leveler of class and caste walls. In the fine words of the late Doctor Nash, "Democracy believes that the downmost man, the man without a grandfather, takes ranks in the spiritual peerage."

Here is something to use—and guard: a priceless but fragile and easily corrupted inheritance. One chief point at which the powerful force of democracy may be in antagonism to the Christian ideal is that it easily degenerates into a blind faith in majorities and in an uncritical following of them. It has a tendency to level down as well as level up, so that the result may be a sub-Christian ethical mediocrity. The tendency of a superficial democracy to level life down to the greatest common denominator has the effect of making a new American Holy Trinity. The ultimate authority is Tom, Dick, and Harry. It has made for conformity and lack of respect for minorities.

So it is with the kindred ideal of equality, an ideal to which there is more evident devotion to-day than to its historically related ideals of liberty and fraternity. It is born of the idea central to Jesus of the fundamental worth of the individual. It has made for respect for human life, a potent force both for justice and sympathy. A distinguished English critic, J. A. Spender, observes: "Equality has real value and meaning for American people. Whatever liberties may have been taken with liberty, equality and fraternity hold their own. Easy familiarity of intercourse, a recognition of the worth of men and women as such, makes an Englishman aware of the extent to which his own country is class-ridden."

Equality has the same easy possibilities of perversion as noted above with democracy. A passion for equality has often been a force running counter to ethical advance. There is a widespread exaltation of equality on a level so low as to leave out cultural and spiritual distinction.

Liberty is another outstanding American ideal. A faith in it and a willingness to sacrifice for it have been prominent through all American history. It has been so easily made a cloak for swarming things—self-interest and license. Yet it is an inevitable corollary to Jesus' sense of man's sonship to God and the sacredness of his personality. A devotion to liberty is Americanism of the most authentic sort. In that devotion Christianity and this frequently outraged American trait must unite to restore civil liberties over large areas where they are constantly infringed. A penetrating European traveler, C. W. Jansen, in his volume, *A Stranger in America*, published early in the last century, cites the following experience as the most illuminating thing in America.

He knocked at the door of an acquaintance and asked the domestic who opened it to him, "Is your master at home?"

"I have no master," was the ready reply.

"Don't you live here?" Mr. Jansen asked.

"I stay here," was the answer.

"And who are you, then?" Jansen pursued.

"Why, I am Mr. ———'s help. I would have you know, man, that I am no servant."

That little conversation on the doorstep epitomized two hundred years of history. In critical and disillusioned days we may easily forget the reality expressed in the inscription carved on the base of the Statue of Liberty in New York harbor, written by Emma Lazarus, a Jewess:

"Give me your tired, your poor,
    Your huddled masses yearning to breathe free,
The wretched refuse of your teeming shore—
    Send these, the homeless, tempest-tost, to me—
I lift my lamp beside the golden door."

Energy! What critic ever denied energy as an American quality? Both those who mock and those who revere do so on the ground of energy. The hero in Eugene O'Neill's "Dynamo" is a typical American in his worship of the machine and in his respect for power. Hugo Münsterberg lists what he calls "self-activity" as one of his three fundamental traits which explain the American. It is in energy that J. Ellis Barker, the noted English economist, finds a large part of "America's secret." He says:

The country was settled by men possessing the conquering spirit and the spirit of leadership. These men fought among themselves, fought the Indians, and conquered the wilderness aroung them. . . . They created a new race, possessed of daring enterprise, of boundless energy, and of the passionate desire for achievement and success. . . . American economic success is less due to the vastness of its natural wealth and to the excellence of its machinery than to the ambition, good sense, ingenuity, and industry of the people and the wisdom and energy of the leaders.

One of the most graphic descriptions of this quality of energy is Sydney Smith's epigram that

"Daniel Webster was a steam engine in trousers."
There are a great many steam engines in trousers
extant in America. We see so much chaos of hustle
and bustle that at times it seems like a million devils
in trousers. Hence the description of America as
the United States as a nation of extraverts. Yet
it would be a distorted vision which would fail to
find in this vast reservoir of energy a force of enormous promise for the establishment of a Christian
social order. Anyone tempted to disparage energy
in itself ought to reread the Gospels. One of the
outstanding impressions made on an open mind is the
degree to which Jesus loved energy. T. R. Glover
has pointed out the extent to which many of the
parables turn on energy, showing how intensely
Jesus admired energy and decision, and what a high
place he gave to them in his valuation of human
qualities. "These are the things that Jesus admires
—in the widow who will have justice (Luke 18. 2);
in the virgins who thought ahead and bought extra
oil (Matt. 25.4); in the vigorous man who found
the treasure and made sure of it (Matt. 13. 44);
in the friend at midnight, who hammered, hammered, hammered, until he got his loaves (Luke
11. 8). Even the bad steward he commends because he definitely put his mind on his situation
(Luke 16. 8)."

When we think of the tasks involved in the making
of a Christlike world, we realize that only a boundless
energy will ever suffice to make even a beginning.
We have the inspiration of achievement where this
prodigious American energy was joined with sympathy to accomplish a great moral end, such as the Bel-
gian relief or, even more impressive, because more

unselfish, the Russian relief.   Undertakings such as
these make clear what a vigorous thrust of energy can
accomplish when giving momentum to ideal ends.   In
this energy is one of the greatest assets in the world
for a Christian order.   Like all power, its value depends on the object to which it attaches itself.   Rufus
Choate said that John Quincy Adams was a "bull-
dog with confused ideas."   That is the liability of tremendous energy.   If the ends which it sets foremost
are the result of confused thinking and unethical
valuation, it can become a massive force destructive
to human welfare.

   Individualism is likewise a deeply engraved trait,
which has found expression in a multitude of cus-
toms and institutions.   Indeed, in some respects it
seems the fundamental American ideal, the right of
the free individual to enjoy the opportunities that
he may face and the necessity for him to meet the
obligations he incurs.   America, as the land of
opportunity, has meant to a large extent, when
translated into realities of economic life, the opportunity for the individual to promote his welfare.
It has been the corner stone of American tradition,
and it is easy to see that it is at once a precious
heritage and a diabolic force in economic exploitation.
It has values closely aligned to the Christian sense
of the worth of the individual.   Yet that feeling for
the supremacy of an individual's rights has been
again and again made equivalent to a religious and
patriotic blessing on the motive of unrestricted economic gain.

   So with two other qualities so commonly called
American—adventurousness and youth.   Adventurousness is a prime requisite if new experiments in

human relations are to be tried. That quality of adventurousness is the one to which the Christian ethic must appeal in its conflict with the inertia of privilege and tradition. Youthfulness as a quality of American life may so manifest itself when focused on high goals as to supply the suppleness, the readiness for the new, the hopefulness necessary for fresh ethical advances. But attached to lower goals it manifests itself as childishness, juvenility, a satisfaction with externals.

Finally, the religious interest in a great majority of American people has been deep, genuine, and pervasive. The foundations of most of the American colonies were laid in religious cement. It is the historians of the United States rather than its preachers who have told most effectively the influence of religion in shaping national character, particularly in supplying the motive power for reforms and ethical advancement. This influence is so evident that a casual survey of it may easily lead one to overestimate its social results. To-day the dangers in connection with the religious heritage are painfully evident: that it may become a surface veneer, a sort of pious embellishment on a pagan life; that it may become for multitudes more what it already is for many, an emotional compensation for failing to take seriously religion's ethical demands, and so an escape into fantasy from harsh reality.

Our chief attention in the rest of this volume will be given to some American trends which are in sharp and deadly conflict with the Christian ethic: externalism induced by the profusion of material things; the mechanization of life as an end in itself; the crude worship of size and the subordination of quality; the prestige of the profit motive and the ascendency of a business philosophy over the whole of life; the impersonal quality of industry and its assault on personality; the deification of salesmanship, the vulgarization by machine-made recreation, the cult of the mental lock step.

To bring the mind of Jesus into the mind of the nation involves two main lines of strategy. The first is to provide new goals for old powers; to direct to high Christian ends the available spiritual and ethical resources which are to be found in deeply rooted American traits. It is substantially the engineer's problem with the Mississippi River, to direct the tremendous force which comes from the streams that drain a continent away from destructive wanderings into channels that make for human welfare. The second task is to keep the best in American character from being thwarted and paralyzed by present powerful trends in the social and industrial world.

The real task of religion in America to-day is shown by the outstanding contrast of our civilization: we have a wonderful resourcefulness in mastering things; we are baffled by human relationships. The first step toward a better order is, in the classic words of Matthew Arnold's definition of culture, "to turn a stream of fresh and free thought upon our stock notions and habits." That we must do in the high faith in the nation expressed in the moving words of John Milton—"A nation should be one huge Christian personage, one mighty growth and stature of an honest man."

CHAPTER III

AMERICAN HERITAGES—
THE LEGACY OF THE PURITAN

AMERICAN history began with two words, *Land Ahead!*

Since those words were first called from the deck of the Santa Maria they have formed a dominant motif of the drama. They were repeated from the crest of the Alleghanies as the first wave of pioneers looked down into the western slopes and valleys. They were shouted from the Mississippi valley as the great exodus across the plains began. The columns pushed ahead under the exultation of that cry, "Land ahead!"

Of all the formative influences on the national mind and character, the land itself is first. It is the old story of Eden repeated in every country; man is formed from the dust of the ground; his particular characteristics derive in real degree from the geographical and geological conditions. This has been true everywhere from Egypt to Southern California. Large place, consequently, must be given to the continent itself as the first factor in the cultural and spiritual heritage of the United States. This heritage of the land is placed prominently in the verses of "America."

"I love thy rocks and rills,
Thy woods and templed hills."

For the rocks and the woods, a panorama three thousand miles long, have had a large determining influence. Indeed, the very air in the Northern part of the United States has made its contribution to the febrile energy of the people.

Applying the terms of the Eden story, it may be said that not only the dust of the ground shaped the character of the American but that particular form of the dust known as boulders in New England and mud in the Mississippi valley. There is a profound fitness in the lyrical tribute paid by Carl Sandburg in his *Abraham Lincoln, the Prairie Years* to the black gumbo mud of Illinois. Soft gumbo mud was one of the spiritual ancestors of Lincoln. It played a large part in shaping the national and moral features of the environment from which Lincoln came—and "trailing clouds of glory" did he come. In other words, there was mud on his boots. The quality of his manhood derived essential characteristics from the great American adventure with the land.

The horizon has been a character-molding influence. The very size and range of the theater in which the plot of history was to be worked out have had a strong influence on the actors. What many European appraisers have failed to see in their shocked disapproval of American morals and manners is that these marks were not so much due to human depravity as to physical geography.

A number of years ago an English valet accompanied his employer on a trip across the United States. He sat for nearly four days on the observation platform of a transcontinental train watching the continent recede from him. These four days he

held his peace.   But somewhere in Nevada he con-
fided to his employer, sitting next to him: "I have
been thinking about Christopher Columbus.   They
have made a great to-do about him discovering
America, but I think it was not so much.   I don't
see how he could help it!"   After a four days' trip
across the continent the discovery of America does
seem a bit obvious.   Many results of the very size
of the United States could not "be helped" either.

Indeed, so great and permanent have been the
influences of the land in American character and
history that a recent attempt has been made to
interpret the whole sweep of national history in
terms of a vast project in the real-estate business.
The author states his theme thus:

In this country all men are realtors.   As a prime symbol of our civilization neither the Pilgrim Father, nor the
pioneer, nor the captain of industry suffices so well as
the real-estate man to explain certain habits of mind,
certain values and inconsistencies of the behavior of the
American people.

And so, beginning with the colonies as real estate
ventures, he finds such features as the present-day
scene as regimented boosting, a faith in progress, and
the spirit of speculation in futures as deriving from
a devotion to increase in land values.   A much more
serious historian, Carl Russell Fish, has thus recognized the same influence:

Land seemed to nearly all Americans the key to happiness.   With a vast majority the desire was for enormous
land to cultivate; with a great number the desire was to
skim the cream of increasing land values.

The real-estate agent was only two jumps behind
Daniel Boone as he crossed the Appalachians.   This

broad theme of the influence of the great heritage
of the land on the character of the people who subdued and occupied it has been treated in many
volumes. Here all that can be done is to list it as
a first inheritance. The consequences of the enormous physical resources stretch into every aspect
of life. The vast task of occupation carved deeply
pioneer traits of character. The immense resources and the scarcity of labor gave incentive to
invention and the use of machinery and the development of the processes of mass production in manufacture. They also led to a continuous search for
cheap labor, with its results in slavery and unrestricted immigration and the consequent mixing
of nationalities in the population.

In a well-known poem the continent is pictured
as saying, "Give me men to match my mountains."
The mountains to some degree helped to create the
man. The spaciousness of America helped to create
a certain spaciousness of character. To some extent
it had also a result of an opposite sort. The demand for intensity of application which subduing a
wilderness enforces resulted in a mental parochialism.
The pioneer farmer was plowing long furrows and
could not look up.

The two strongest historical influences in the
making of American mentality have been the Puritan and the Pioneer. These are the gemini, the
twins in the national pantheon who created broad
streams of influences. They are represented by two
statues. One is the familiar statue by Saint Gaudens,
in Springfield, Massachusetts, designed to present
an ideal picture of Deacon Chapin, a prominent
figure in the First Church of Springfield in the early

days. But it is generally called, as it well deserves to be, "The Puritan." There he stands with his high-crowned, broad rimmed hat, jerkin and knickerbockers and heavy-toed shoes. A broad cape is thrown around his shoulders. A thick staff is in one hand; in the other is a massive Bible. The square jaw gives to the face an impressive determination and courage.

In Kansas City is a statue of the other figure, "The Pioneer." "Land ahead," is written on his features. He carries not a staff but a gun. He is the hero of the greatest trek in human history.

A strange destiny has overtaken both these figures. Once they were the heroes of the story; now they are the villains.

We have had much critical scrutiny of the historical influence of both the Puritan and Pioneer. It has had a sound historical basis, but on that foundation many fantastic superstructures of interpretation have been raised. Many have taken the formula that some of our most unpleasant characteristics have been the heritage of the Puritan and the Pioneer and have shaken it as a dog shakes a bone. These two figures have become the new national scapegoats. There is hardly a feature of present-day life which has not been ascribed to one of them, frequently to both. These interpreters have gone on the theory that anything worth doing at all is worth doing well.

Someone has said of the psychologist of to-day that all he needs is a rat and a formula. Give to certain historians, in like manner, a buckle from the shoe of some Puritan worthy and a single page from the Bay State Psalm Book and they will reconstruct the entire industrial history of the nation.

Samuel M. Crothers says that "when a new idea gets into an unfurnished mind it has the time of its life." Certainly, the comparatively new idea of the economic interpretation of the Puritan and pioneer has had a rollicking and exuberant time in many uncluttered minds.

With this warning, therefore, let us look at the first figure, the Puritan. The Puritan has good cause to make the old prayer, "I can take care of my enemies, save me from my friends." For it is the uncritical adulation, the stereotyped, romantic idealization of the Puritan which is partly responsible for his present plight as the arch villain.

Sound historical study has greatly changed the conception of the influence of the Puritan on national traits and particularly on the economic traits of the country. But it is obvious that not all the changed position of the Puritan in the national mind is due to sound historical study. The Puritan has been the most lampooned figure in history. But it is doubtful if the Golden Age of caricature, represented by Butler's *Hudibras*, can match in achievements that of our day, when the Puritan has been set up as the symbol to be attacked by all the resources commanded by the opponents of prohibition.

It is one of the ironies of history that the Puritan, with his mug of ale and his enjoyment of "rum and true religion," should be the accepted symbol of prohibition. It is a major tragedy of the present day that one of the noblest figures of history, a creative influence in American history, should be to millions only a subject for caricature. For caricature destroys the power to appreciate the thing derided. As though to illustrate the effect which this orgy of caricature has on an unfurnished mind, Irvin Cobb plumbs the depths of an impressive ignorance and draws up the generalization that "the landing of the Pilgrims was the greatest misfortune in American history." The Puritan has become the great rubber stamp of our time. This current caricature is thus appropriately described by a wet newspaper: "From the gaunt stove-pipe hat to the stealthy gum shoes it is a masterpiece of suggestive caricature. The cunning, shifty eyes and eager, frosty nose; the lean and shaven jowl; the scrawny neck and sanctimonious cravat; the chapped wrists and bony, prehensile fingers; the lugubrious umbrella and the dismal coat—how vivid and merciless the lampoon! Intolerance, illiberalism, mean-spirited instincts of spying and snooping; craftiness, stupidity, cruelty, hypocrisy—all are there in searing clarity of line."

That effective word in the last line "sear" is a good one except for the omission of one letter—it ought to be "smear." For that is what it is. The ability to smear has never been rated high in art, especially in that difficult form of art historical portraiture.

Another cause leading to a new estimate of Puritan influence is of a vastly different sort. It is found in the study of the economic influence of Protestantism, particularly the Calvinistic and Puritan influence. This has come through the studies of Max Webber and R. H. Tawney. It is particularly through Tawney and his *Religion and the Rise of Capitalism* that the results of this study have been made influential among the English-speaking peoples. Reinhold Niebuhr, in *Does Civilization Need Religion?* has also brought the issues involved into the thinking of a large number of people in this country. Whether one adopts the whole thesis of Tawney in all its details or not, none can deny that he has thrown a flood of light on the relationship between Puritanism and the ethical problems of industrialism.

But even the fresh emphasis on the economic influences of Puritanism and its incentive in developing the economic virtues ought not to blind us to other influences as well.

President James L. McConaughy of Wesleyan University has well said that "moderns are often so critical of the Puritan finger-prints that they forget the foot-prints." Pervasive and abiding has been the religious influence. The Puritan did a lasting service in making religion a formative influence in American character and history. Make all the subtractions from the distinctive religious influence necessary, modify the eulogy as we must, yet there remains a broad and strong stream of religious influence which has given a lasting cast to American character. The central conviction of the Puritan, that of life shaped by the unchanging purpose of a sovereign God, has ramified out into all areas of life. It was a narrow conception of God. Many of the most significant portions of the New Testament remained to him a closed book. The picture of God in Jesus Christ never came out of the fog into clear focus or dominating influence. Distinctive New Testament virtues and experiences such as joy and the central attitude of love were largely out

of the picture.   But the strong sense of God's greatness and man's accountability to him has been a
major influence.   Puritanism as an attitude rather
than an institution has been well described in the
words of Stuart P. Sherman:

> Dissatisfaction with the past, courage to break sharply
> from it, a vision of a better life, readiness to accept dis-
> cipline in order to attain that better life, and a serious
> desire to make that better life prevail—a desire reflecting
> at once his sturdy individualism and his clear sense for
> the need of social solidarity.

In these essential features of Protestantism we
have its high sense of the dignity and seriousness of
life, its idealism and energy.

The theology of Calvinism, with the rights of man
thought of as granted by a sovereign God, has had
immeasurable results for liberty and democracy.
The Puritan is a natural republican, says Tawney.
James I of England, by an unintentional insight,
gave wide expression to this truth when he said,
"Presbyterianism is no religion for a gentleman."
James knew what he was talking about.   Both he
and his mother had had a various and compre-
hensive experience of Presbyterianism, and James,
of course, was right.   Calvinism was no religion for a
gentleman.   Calvinism, in spite of its conception of
predestination, was an open union, and James be-
longed to a closed one—the Amalgamated Order of
Kings and Nobles.   Calvinism carried in its very
heart the conviction not only that a cat may look
at a king, but that a man may look at a king, straight
in the eye by virtue of his common manhood.   More
than that, he could plant his foot on the neck of a

king, if that seemed to be the foreordained place
to plant it at the moment.

In the Calvinistic and Puritan heritage there is a
strangely mixed double strain—that of individualism
and also a strong sense of communal responsibility.
From this comes the contradictory character of much
of the Puritan heritage.   This double strain is to be
found in the impetus which the Puritan gave to his
idea of material success as a sanctified duty, and
also the urge to improve the life of the community,
which has been a powerful influence contributory to
our modern social movements.   In this latter respect there is a strong distinction between Lutheran-
ism and Calvinism.   Luther accepted much more
readily than Calvin the limitation of the areas in
which religion should apply in life.   Calvin's conception of God, which influences the whole Puritan
movement, had a practical result in the conviction
of the duty of the individual to further the work of
God in the world about him.   The Puritan had a
strong sense of social mission.   The prophet of
social Christianity to-day who refuses to admit that
there are two separate spheres of action for religion,
and who stresses the right of God to dominate every
aspect of life, is taking a position akin to a widely
influential Puritan conviction.   The Puritan in New
England was led by a purpose of establishing a
commonwealth into the very foundations of which
was to be built the righteousness of God.   From
this conception is to be traced much of that ideal
earnestness which flowered in American life from
1830-1850.

Coupled with this there went, of course, the
emphasis on individualism which has left a decidedly

mixed heritage.   Yet, while we recognize the impetus
which that individualism has given to the selfish
motives of modern business, the finer aspects of it
must not be dropped from view.   There was a sense
of independence of conviction, which is greatly needed
in our present heyday of standardization.   It is obvious, in addition, that theocratic discipline helped
to inculcate that moderation and restriction of in-
dulgence of appetite which has deeply influenced
our national life.

The present generation has the material for a
clearer understanding of the sources in the Puritan
tradition of many of our more characteristic traits
and reactions, which have determined in part the
attitude of the middle class to society and the state.

As we have already said, this tendency has been
carried to ridiculous lengths by many dexterous interpreters. One of the most delightful absurdities—idio-
cies would not be too strong a word—to be found in
the amazing "intuitions" recorded in Count Keyserling's voluminous book *America Set Free* is an
example of this.   Keyserling says that one subject
which awaits the attention of history and psychology is the American cocktail. "It is certainly
one of the most extraordinary inventions ever made,"
he declares, "in that it numbs instead of stimulates.
Its essence is the mixture of the incongruous and the
incompatible. I think there is a very profound
intention underlying this: the cocktail is intended
to do harm and not to please the taste. It is, in a
word, a somewhat eccentric expression of Puritanism."

At any rate, such a profound insight is a very
characteristic expression of Keyserling. It reminds

us of the definition of intuition as "that power which enables a person to see through a stone wall to what isn't on the other side." It is the profusion of such intuitions, doubtless, which led John Dewey to observe that the first letter of Keyserling's name should be a "G" instead of a "K."

The thesis developed by the most serious study of the economic influences of Puritanism is well expressed in a compact sentence of Lewis Mumford: "All the habits that Puritanism developed, its emphasis on industry, upon self-help, upon thrift, upon the evils of idleness, upon the worthlessness and wickedness of the arts, were so many gratuitous contributions to the industrial revolution."

The general thesis of the changes in religious and political thinking brought by the Reformation is familiar. The first thorough exposition in English of the economic results of the emergence of Protestantism was that of Tawney. He has traced the results of the passing of business and economic life out of the control of the medieval church. Before the Reformation, the canon law of the church was supposed to be the ethical authority under which business was to be conducted. Trade then, of course, was on a much more modest scale, and commerce, in addition to the handicap of both means of transportation and money system, also labored under a good deal of suspicion that it was liable to be tainted with the evil of mammon.

In the canon law there were stressed the enormity of the sin of avarice, the duty of setting a just price and not what one could get under the stress of necessity, and the wickedness of usury; that is, of making money out of lending your neighbor some-

thing of which he had need, though recent studies
have shown that these ideals and laws were continually violated in practice—not least by the church
itself.

To the credit of the medieval church it must be
said that it attempted, in theory at least, to bring
the economic life under the control of moral law—
an attitude which modern Christianity has largely
abandoned.

Into this situation came the Reformation and
the growth of Protestantism. The emphasis on the
right and necessity of individual judgment natu-
rally opposed the unquestioning acceptance of the
authority of the church. With the results of this
individual judgment in the divisive splitting up into
sects and the rise of nationalism and democracy we
are not here primarily concerned.

A similar result took place in the economic field.
With the breakdown of the social control of business, the duty of the individual to make a success
took precedence over the duty of obeying the moral
law in business in the interest of society.

In Tawney's words, the Puritan in the world became one who, "tempered by self-examination, self-
discipline, self-control, was a practical ascetic whose
victories were won not in the cloister but on the
battlefield, in the counting house and in the market."
In this process there arose the tendency of Protestantism to stress the economic virtues of integrity, hard work, temperance, efficiency, and enterprise in the individual rather than those canons of
the moral law which, to some degree at least, pro-
tected society, such as the warning against usury
and the doctrine of a just price. This tendency

was greatly increased by Calvin's treatise written to show the justice of charging interest.

Here was a tendency which contributed largely along with other factors, such as the progress of natural sciences and the opening up of the sea routes to America and the East, to the rise of modern capitalistic civilization. Here also—and this is the heart of our present theme—were influences which put the essential Christian virtues such as love, humility, self-sacrifice, and brotherhood into the background and threw the economic virtues which did not retard the progress of capitalism but, rather, forwarded it, into the foreground. From this flows much of the impotence of Christianity in the nineteenth century as a social force.

In the theology of Puritanism there are elements from which this impetus to the aggressive and materialistic drive of personality are logical results. In its doctrine of divine election Calvinism exalted the will. It was the Will of God which was made the central fact of life, but from an exaltation of the Will of God an inevitable result is a corresponding exaltation of the will of the individual.

One might easily think that the doctrine of predestination would make for a resignation in the individual, for a lassitude, for a careless fatalism—all the things that are distinctly not the mark of Puritanism. But such an idea would leave out of account a natural and contrary result of a strong feeling of the sovereignty of God. In that sense of sovereignty the believer exulted. It was a controlling idea so massive and high that it quickened the initiative, the energy and will of the believer. It was the Old Testament rather than the New

which shaped the Puritan's view of life. From the
Old Testament was accepted the view of prosperity
as a mark of divine favor. Prosperity thus came to
be, not the *ground* of election (Calvin strongly
asserted that good works could not purchase election), but it became in common view a *mark* of election. Consequently, by material progress man made
his "calling and election sure" to his own conscience.

The Puritan had the hope that he was of the elect.
Hence it was his duty to prove it by his prosperity.
He was probably elect anyhow, hence God ought to
shower gifts upon him. Thus the idea that merit
and riches were to be identified became a controlling
one even where it did not receive definite and conscious expression. The gospel of work, the duty
of self-advancement, became articles of working
faith in the acceptance of material success as evidence of divine election. In this working faith there
lie the roots of much American aggressiveness. A
religious backing is given to the motive of "getting
on."

With the stress of man's duty to add to the glory
of God came the practical acceptance of material
progress as an addition to and an expression of that
glory. The great protagonist of Puritan theology
in New England, Jonathan Edwards, is known in
America for his sermon on "Sinners in the Hands of
an Angry God" even more than for his part in the
"Great Awakening." There was another element
in Edwards' theology which, while overlooked, has
left large influence. That element is indicated in
his words, "God in seeking his glory seeks the good
of his creatures; because the emanation of his glory
(which he seeks and delights in, as he delights in

himself, and his own eternal glory) inspires the communicated excellency and happiness of his creatures." This inspired "excellency and happiness of his creatures" as being part of the glory of God was a powerful urge to the high duty of getting on. The primacy of will, of intellect, and emotions was a practical result of the stress on the sovereignty of God and resulted in a concerted sense of purpose. Man's glorification of God is to be crystallized in a life of thrift, sobriety, and expanding energy, in which the will drives its possessor relentlessly and toil becomes a high virtue in life, a sort of "sacrament."

When these inner urges and cast of mind were developed at the same time that the measureless resources of a virgin continent were opened up, it is not hard to understand the impetus given to the acquisitive instincts. From the exaltation of will power and its gospel of success comes much of the seamy side of individualism. When the acquisitive instincts and economic virtues were baptized by Puritanism it was a thorough job—"baptism by immersion." The stage was set for the ascendency of business as the dominant interest of life; for the individual exploitation which accompanied the Machine Age; for the goal of "getting on" in its place, as the practical, if not the proclaimed chief end of man. This mind-set has contributed greatly to the fundamental unethical character of much of our civilization.

Not least among the heritages left by these conceptions and their practical results in character was a church unable to bring the ethical insight which would have been a challenge to the new industrialism as it developed. It had within itself no definite rebuke to the anti-Christ of the new forms and technique of greed. The ethical protests of a church dominated by Puritan traits largely exhausted themselves in matters of individual conduct and personal morals. The revivalism which followed Puritanism did not face the real economic issues, for the good reason that Protestantism itself had become the stronghold of anti-Christian attitudes, motives, and practices. The Protestant Church at large could see, for instance, the wickedness of a man like Jim Fisk, but it was more appalled by his sexual immorality than by the immorality of manipulating the stock market. It could not see with equal clearness the immorality of a man like Fisk's partner in crime, Daniel Drew.

There is large truth in Agnes Repplier's playful statement that "America has invested her religion as well as her morality in sound, income-paying securities." Indeed, we may say of the Puritan baptism of economic success: "If you would see its monument, look around you at the brutalities resulting from the unrestrained acceptance of profit motive in industry!"

CHAPTER IV

AMERICAN HERITAGES—
THE FRONTIER INHERITANCE

To try to suggest in a compact form the influence of the frontier and the pioneer mentality would be to undertake to tell the whole story of American history.

Two of the keenest observers who ever studied the United States have emphasized the frontier as the key to the history and development of the people. One was a Frenchman and the other was an American. One wrote in the early stages of the Western movement; the other just at the close of the free land in 1890, which brought the frontier definitely to a close. The Frenchman was De Tocqueville. One of the most striking passages in his *Democracy in America* is that in which he discovers the "poetry and destiny of America in a romance of a moving frontier; in the vision which led the pioneer on his conquering way across the plains and mountains toward the Pacific, contending with an endless wilderness which was matched only by his ambition." At the latter end of the period Frederick J. Turner, then professor in the University of Wisconsin, read a paper in 1893 before the American Historical Association on "The Significance of the Frontier in American History." It is no exaggeration to say that Professor Turner's paper did more to influence historical research and writing in America than any other production. His theme was a double one: first, that "The existence of an area of free land, its continuous recession and the advance of the American settlement westward explain American development"; and, second, "To the frontier the American intellect owes its striking characteristics." Professor Turner's work gives a clear exposition of the roots of many of the ethical problems in the present industrial order in America. For Turner and the company who have followed in his train have shown that the qualities developed in frontier life of three thousand miles in space and three hundred years in time have carried over into the Machine Age when the land frontier is gone, and into areas of the population and fields of action not primarily engaged in subduing the land.

With many of the influences of the frontier on the development of history we are not here primarily concerned. Among these is its contribution to the making of the nation. In a real sense the creation of the nation is the achievement of the frontier. The nation found itself in the spirit of nationality which came from newly carved out and settled States beyond the Alleghanies. The real allegiance of these new territories was not to any particular State along the Atlantic seaboard, but, rather, to the national government which had given them their land and called them into being. Through these new territories the wavering federal government was strengthened to dominate the sectional interest of the original colonies. The bread cast on the waters reappeared after not very many days. Again, in the struggle in the Civil War it was the West which turned the balance in favor of the Union.

If the frontier can be said to have made the nation, its life and conditions went far to make a new people. Beyond the Alleghanies was the first real melting pot. We are tempted to locate it at Ellis Island. In reality it was first located in the Ohio valley, and a composite people was fused out of various sectional and national elements.

The very conditions of life inevitably made for a growth of democracy. Where the very survival of life depended on strength and courage, the worth of the common man received strong emphasis. We are accustomed to trace the spread of democracy to the cabin of the Mayflower. It had another and even stronger source in another sort of cabin— the pioneer cabin on the edge of the wilderness. In American history the spread of democracy is like the old Greek fable of Antæus, the wrestler whose strength was renewed whenever his feet touched the ground. Democracy waxed strong on the land. Notice that a new spirit had been brought into being and was served in the election of Andrew Jackson to the presidency in 1828. As a background for observing the rise of mental qualities of Americans which came from the frontier some broad elementary aspects of the picture must be kept in mind. First among these are the vast dimensions of the material conquest. The Western march of the population was a vastly different thing from the sweep of great hordes across a continent such as has happened so often in history, which Ellsworth Huntington calls "the pulse of Asia," whose beating was felt in successive spurts which threw invasions from Asia into Europe. The pioneers in America undertook to carry a whole civilization with them.

To cavil at the pioneers, as Lewis Mumford does in *The Golden Day*, for giving so little attention to culture and becoming so absorbed in material enterprise, is to forget the prodigious demands of the physical task and to be unfair historically.

Mr. Mumford says: "Thoreau, in his life and letters, shows what the pioneer movement might have become if this great migration had sought culture instead of material conquest and intensity of life rather than mere extension over the continent." It is very easy to administer such a rebuke from the luxurious armchair provided by twentieth-century America. One suspects, however, that if Mr. Mumford had trekked his way across the Alleghanies after a Canestoga wagon at the beginning of the nineteenth century or had followed the Oregon Trail to the far West in the middle of the century, he would have found it rather easier to understand why "this great migration" was more occupied in material conquest than in the pursuit of culture.

It must be remembered, moreover, that the frontier movement was a conquest by individuals. There were no State subsidies, no military guard, no help but in themselves. It was first and last a family enterprise. Though large trains of immigrants traveled together over the Oregon and Santa Fé trails, and across the unmarked plains hundreds of covered wagons frequently moved in parade, the source and momentum of the exploit was in individuals.

It is also true that life on the frontier gave rise to a mental expression of co-operation and helpfulness. Yet deeper than that was its development of a marked strain of self-initiative and self-reliance for all that this meant for good or ill in a later generation.

It must be remembered also that this westward thrust was made by a selected people. Just as the hazard of crossing the Atlantic and establishing oneself in the wild conditions of the New World exercised a selection among those who made the venture in colonial days, so the frontier called to itself the adventurers, the resolute, those dissatisfied with their prospects in the more static life of the seaboard. The company thus called were the best and the worst; but they were united by a common trait—the daring to look with level eyes at danger and a readiness for the new. This moving column of people could say with Ulysses:

> "I am become a name
> For always roaming with a hungry heart."

Moving day is as characteristically an American holiday as the Fourth of July.

Professor Carl Russell Fish likens this restlessness to the search for the Holy Grail. "The desire for adventure," he says, "the belief that it was manly for a youth to fare forth after his future, the conviction that there was some Holy Grail to reward the disinterested, was at this period (1830-1850) touching actually a larger percentage of Americans than at any other time."

The frontier was a fresh experiment in eugenics in which people were bred for qualities making for survival amidst rough and dangerous conditions. That the experiment was a success is shown by the survival of the qualities after the original experiment was over.

The conditions of the material conquest bred

highly selected qualities. The traits of personality, temperament, and character encouraged and fostered were those which made for success on the frontier. Other traits, no matter how valuable they might be in themselves or in another environment, were minimized or sloughed off. Individual activity, inventiveness, self-reliance, endurance under back-breaking toil, optimism—all these were the inevitable product of the pioneer's life. It is a heritage which Frederick J. Turner has put into one striking and inclusive sentence in which is distilled a hundred years of history. "That coarseness and strength combined with acuteness and acquisitiveness; that practical, inventive turn of mind quick to find expedients; that masterful grasp of material things, lacking in the artistic but powerful to effect great ends; that restless, nervous energy; that dominant individualism working for good and evil, and withal that buoyancy and exuberance which comes from freedom—these are the traits of the frontier or traits called out elsewhere because of the existence of the frontier."

As we have seen in the case of the Puritan a new scrutiny of the ethical heritage which the American people have in the ascendency of these qualities, ought not to obscure the great ethical and spiritual resources which the pioneer has left in American life. A naïve glorification, of which we have surfeit, should not blind us to the idealism of the pioneer or his development of forces available for Christian purposes. The quest for material advantage, the land hunger and all the effects which flowed from it, were moving forces in conquering the wilderness, and in them there was a real idealism. There was a high zest of adventure engendering qualities congenial to the highest moral uses—a search for liberty and freedom of opportunity, a high estimate of the common man, a willingness to sacrifice for a better stake in life for one's family, including education and comfort; a faith in the future.   There was a very real idea of the long stretches of vacant lands as a possible theater for a new order of life (a strain that occurs again and again in the personal records and other literature of the time and movement), and a patriotic conception of pushing out the national domains and adding to the greatness of the nation.

Yet it was a strangely mixed heritage.   The liability side of the balance sheet is heavy.   Pioneer people were of necessity practical.   They prided themselves most on their practicalness.   The immediate, the concrete, the tangible, occupied the largest part of their interests.   The result was a limitation of life, an acceptance of many limits and walls for their interests, the subordination of the adventure of living to the machinery of keeping alive.   This left the heritage of emphasis on "things," a characteristic which leads foreigners glibly to call us a "nation of extraverts," in which the realities of the objective scene are the supreme concern of life.   It has made for a one-sided preoccupation with practical contrivances.   From this derives the tendency to externalism in the American people, the unproclaimed feeling that life consists in a multitude of things, Jesus or anyone else to the contrary notwithstanding.   This has made very stony soil for Jesus' central emphasis on the primacy of the inner life.

A far more perverse heritage is the stress on

individualism given by the frontier experience. As we have seen, this stress was not undiluted. Frontier life by its very risks and dangers forced men to be companionable. Sticking together not only had its advantages, it was frequently a very condition of survival. But individualism was far more vigorously stimulated than co-operation and more deeply engraved into character and more forcibly expressed in economic life.

The emphasis was on individual success. The career that was open to talent, the resentment of social control which would limit private accumulations, the consequent play of competitive spirit, were the ruling forces. These are perilous traits to be developed and their persistence has done much to augment the selfish grasping of a later industrial age. This individualism explains the attitude toward government; the people of the frontier wanted its help where possible profit was concerned; they insisted on its keeping hands off when the laying on of hands would interfere with profit. That is a dominant attitude of business to-day.

This individualism has engendered carelessness of the rights and welfare of others as well as the waste of natural resources, which are so tragic an expression of the frontier spirit.

V. L. Parrington says in this connection: "The pioneers interpreted the Declaration of Independence to mean the natural right of every free citizen to satisfy his acquisitive instinct by exploiting the natural resources in the satisfaction of his shrewdness."

One far-reaching result has been the prestige of the sacred gospel of success. Here, as in other respects, the pioneer heritage combined with that of the Puritan to give a strong bent to American character. The conception that it is the chief duty of man to "get on" had both the Puritan and Pioneer as its god-parents at its baptism. When the last frontier was reached and there was no more free land in any considerable quantity, the energy which had been developed turned back to find other spheres for its employment. The qualities nourished in one hundred years of frontier exploits found a new theater in the growing industrialism. Buffalo Bill moved to Pittsburgh. A new industrial setting was marked by a ruthless exploitation, an unscrupulous disregard for human factors as long as the main chance was seized, a commercial massacre which was the counterpart of a thousand frontier dramas and fights.

One special aspect of this exaltation of success is the fostering of the speculative mania by the frontier conditions and its selective development of qualities. Wall Street is a continuation of the Oregon Trail. The optimistic temper of the new frontier readily passed over into speculation.

Colonel Sellers and his watchword, "There's millions in it," was not a libel; his imagination merely operated on a somewhat larger scale than that of his neighbors. In so vast a scene the traditional economy which reckoned in terms of use and the normal return on investment was changed to one of quick speculative profit; a change which the system of paper money intensified and accelerated. The spirit of hurry, itself partly a consequence of pioneer optimism, contributed to the prevalence of the speculative temper. This trait was never more evident in its baneful results than in the frenzied stock market operations of 1929.

It may seem a long way from the frontiersmen plowing their acres to the stock market, but there is a straight path between them. The elevation of the shining prize of "getting something for nothing" helped to create a major ethical liability for to-day, and a baffling obstacle to making Christianity dominant in the life of our time.

Mixed in with these was that special form of heritage which may be called "boom-town" optimism. At first glance optimism may seem to resemble the high Christian virtue of faith. Certainly, the optimism of the middle west in frontier days was "a conviction of things not seen!" Surely, it was a rare form of vision which could see a golden future for a typical frontier town, Chicago, in this portrait of its childhood taken in 1840: "It stank to heaven, this mudhole in the prairie on the banks of garlic creek; was full of slaughter houses, tanneries, soap and candle works. Pigs romped in the puddles; cows slept on the side streets, and for miles in every direction was a solid mass of mud. Arriving travelers walked up to their shins in it, beside coaches up to their hubs. Thieves, swindlers were everywhere."

But this "boom-town" optimism has been an ample cloak for a multitude of sins. It has contributed to the worship of meaningless bigness; to the substitution of quantity for quality, to the toleration of many social wrongs as long as they are good for business. It ministers to complacency, to the vicious regimentation of ideas; it has been an

effective drug to civic conscience, and has helped
to promulgate the doctrine of infallibility of business.   In other words, it has been a fruitful source
of characteristic moral diseases of American cities.

Waste has always accompanied the pioneer trail.
There is an old fairy story of "The Enchanted
Penny," the story of a magical purse from which the
lucky possessor could take out a penny always to
find there another penny left.   The typical American attitude to national resources has been to regard
the land as an enchanted purse, which could be
plundered at will without exhausting its wealth.
That criminal recklessness is the cause of many
shortages which are faced to-day.

We have burned more forests, dug more coal,
squandered more gas and oil than any people in the
world.   America First!   The pioneer heritage cannot be charged with the whole appalling total of
waste so characteristic of America, but it must bear
the burden of a large part of it.

Here, then, is a cluster of influences superbly
fitted to the service of the profit motive in industry
and business.   It has been ready at hand to serve
the hard drive for material prosperity, the im-
patience of social restraint and the ascendency of
industrial autocracy in the foreground of our life.

The industrial development in the United States
has gone on long enough to be considered a heritage
of our own generation from the past.   Not from a
far past; but its machinery and the problems which
arise from it have not originated with us.   They
have been increasing since the Civil War.

The present tendency among historians in inter-
preting the significance of the Civil War is not to look

at it as primarily a struggle of slavery, not even over
the preservation of the Union as much as a clash
between an industrial and an agricultural order. The
victory was the victory of the machine, or, as some
have expressed it, "the abolition of an old form of
slavery by a new one." At any rate, the period following the Civil War marks the change from an
America dominated by rural and provincial culture
to one dominated by a machine-driven industrialism.

The ascendency of the machine and the industrial
civilization built upon it have brought profound
changes in the mental and social make-up of the
people. It is unquestionably too much to say, as
one critic does of the period between the close of
the Civil War and the World War, "Business was
the only activity it respected. Comfort was the
only result it sought." But it is only a mild statement of the truth to say that the ascendency of
industrialism founded on science and the machine
has brought a new pattern of life into existence.
There is no need to labor this obvious truth. It fs
suggested in two pictures.

Professor A. M. Schlesinger has vividly set forth
the extent to which Abraham Lincoln would be a
Rip Van Winkle amidst the physical changes which
the machine and industrial development have
brought to the world to-day.

If Lincoln were to return now and walk about Washington, he would be surprised and bewildered by the
things he would see. Buildings more than three or four
stories high would be new. The plate-glass show windows of the stores, the electric street-lighting, the moving-
picture theaters, the electric elevators in the buildings,
and especially the big department stores would be things
in his day unknown. The smooth-paved streets and

cement sidewalks would be new to him. The fast-moving electric street cars and motor vehicles would fill him with wonder. Even a boy on a bicycle would be a curiosity. Entering the White House, someone would have to explain to him such commonplaces of modern life as sanitary plumbing, steam heating, friction matches, telephones, electric lights, the victrola, and even the fountain pen. In Lincoln's day plumbing was in its beginning, coal-oil lamps and gas-jets were just coming into use, and the steel pen had only recently superseded the quill pen. The steel rail, the steel bridge, high-powered locomotives, refrigerator cars, artificial ice, the cream separator, the twine binder, the caterpillar tractor, money orders, the parcel post, rural free delivery, the cable, the wireless, gasoline engines, repeating rifles, dynamite, submarines, airplanes—these and hundreds of other inventions now in common use were all alike unknown.

The change from life molded in its form and thinking by a rural economy to an urban industry is presented with stimulating first aid to the imagination by Stephen Leacock's parody on "An Elegy in a Country Churchyard" which he calls "An Elegy Near a City Freight Yard." The well-known lines of Gray, which are rooted in our minds, supply the contrast by which to measure the transformation:

"The factory whistles blow across the way,
    Some cattle in a freight car still I see,
The employees have finished for the day,
    And there is no one on the street but me.

"Now they have lighted the electric light,
    And all the people in the stores have gone,
Except the cop on duty for the night,
    And round the corner p'haps a motor horn.

"Save that from yonder little railway tower
　　The switchman now and then is heard complain,
When someone in a motor at this hour
　　Compels him to lift up his gates again. . . ."

The lea and lowing herd have given place to the macadam and the limousine.

The world has long since recovered from the first demented intoxication with which our forefathers in England and America greeted the machine; a delirium which almost made, in the time-honored phrase, "a god from the machine." The consequences of that worship have remained as a shaping force in our day.

An acute critic at the time of the opening of the Crystal Palace Exposition in London in 1850, pointed out that a great many people were liable to mistake the Crystal Palace for the kingdom of God. That confused identification was one of the root causes of the World War. A great many people in the mood of superficial optimism saw, and many still see, a heaven built on scientific knowledge harnessed to machinery.

The prophecy recorded in the New Testament as being made to Peter has a very close, though wholly unintended, application to the change brought in man's life by a machine-driven industrialism. "When thou wast young, thou girdest thyself, and walkedst whither thou wouldest; but when thou shalt be old, thou shalt stretch forth thy hands, and another shall gird thee, and carry thee whither thou wouldest not" (John 21.18).

That surely is what has happened on a large scale to man. Forces which he has brought into being have gotten beyond his control and have girded

him and are carrying him into the accomplishment
of purposes which are not his own. The industrialism which was called in as a servant of life has in
many ways become its master. Man has had to
conform his life to the demands and needs of the
Frankenstein monster he has brought into being.

Three large results, among others, of far-reaching
ethical significance come from this.

One of them is the impersonalization of life which
the machine promotes. Inevitably it substitutes for
the ethical quality preserved in face-to-face relations
between men the irresponsibility which grows up
when that relation becomes impersonal. It is
inevitable that the impersonal attitude so dominant
in a subjugation of material things should carry
over as the dominant attitude in relation to human
beings.

Another result which has not received so much
attention is that living in an industrial order which
continually denies and thwarts the essential human
relations between men makes a real belief in a personal God more and more difficult. Indeed, as many
have pointed out, the most formidable obstacle to a
Christian theism to-day is not in the intellectual
difficulties involved in a belief in a personal, loving
God. It is, rather, the psychological and moral
difficulty of holding that belief in a vital way in a
social and economic environment in which it is
continually denied.

A third result is the extent to which science and
industry have made possible the ascendency of
business as the controlling factor in life.

Industrialism did not create the profit motive, but
it has put into its hand undreamed of powers. It is

a commonplace to say that our modern world through
its scientific inventions has given to man new ears
and new eyes. His hearing and his vision can now
be extended around the world. It is also true this
same mastery of mechanical processes gives new
powers to greed. It has given to it big paws with a
longer reach, more powerful muscles, and sharper
teeth.

Another factor in the making of characteristic
American mentality which must be at least named
is the growth of cities; the urbanization of the mind
of the people of the United States. The full consequence of this cannot be told in figures, striking as
they are. In the days of the Revolution 97 per cent.
of the people lived on the farm; only 3 per cent.
in cities. To-day scarcely more than 35 per cent.
work in the fields and not more than 45 per cent.
are directly dependent on agricultural processes for
a living. Yet Harriet Martineau, in her visit to the
United States in 1836, was greatly concerned for the
future because so many young men were leaving the
city for the country! How much the urbanization
of the country has been accelerated by the motor
car is an interesting field for speculation. Mr.
Charles Merz says that one of the epochal dates
in American history was the night when Henry Ford
first drove his sputtering car, which was put together out of assorted junk piles, around the block,
for then, he says, was settled the struggle between
the country and the town. The coughing engine
was announcing in a new guttural language that a
rural and an urban culture could not exist side by
side in this country. The motor car has carried
the ideas and standards of the city into the whole

countryside. It was a new mechanical version of Lincoln's axiom that "a house divided against itself cannot stand."

A British observer, Douglas Woodruff, surveying this "America on wheels," confesses:

It will not surprise me much if the private home is abolished in America to give place to the residential car, so that the American soul may find a final happiness and men may be born in cars and live there, wed there, die in them and be cremated in the engine without ever having to put a foot on the ground. And so will arise a new race to take the place of the centaur of old, or, as the centaurs were half men and half horse, so will these be half men and half motor car.

The percentage of urban population is much higher in England than in the United States, but it is a question whether the urbanization of the United States in the sense of the city furnishing a pattern of culture for the whole nation is not more complete in the United States. Among the primary results of this are the draining off of a large part of the population, particularly the younger section, from the country to the cities. This domination of the city ways and standards, style and ideas is also the source of the formidable standardizing influences. Mass standards are given enormous and almost irresistible prestige, which is fast destroying the distinctive character and the sectional flavor of the rural regions, with all which that means for a fruitful variety and independence in the mental and moral life of the nation. One special result of large importance of the urbanization process lies in the fact that historically the strength of organized religion has been in the rural regions. With the constantly increasing dominance of the city in ways of thinking and living has come a lessening of that historic strength, with the added result that Protestantism in America, being largely based on a rural culture and environment, has been ill adapted to cope with the rapidly changing environment in the city.

Let us glance at another large influence which has left a heritage. The prestige of the scientific movement is, of course, not in any sense peculiarly American. It marks the whole temper of the Western world. But it is a definite and powerful element in the intellectual heritage of the present day in the United States. Autocratic authority in religion and morals is a Humpty Dumpty which has fallen off the high wall never to be replaced again. In many respects that is a real asset both for religion and ethics. It is a liability to the extent that it has created a tendency among multitudes to throw out of consideration everything which is not arrived at by the processes of scientific measurement.

Dr. John B. Watson's slogan, "Feed me on facts," has been industriously adopted, with the narrowest possible interpretation of a fact as being something which can be weighed and measured in a laboratory or seen through a microscope or a telescope. The practical results of the scientific method in the mastery of nature, its ministry to comfort, has given it an enormous prestige in the minds of the present generation. Here, obviously, is "success." This undeniable success has given rise to a faith in science which has made for a very unscientific use of its prestige. This faith lies at the heart of our secular civilization.

It has created a mood and temper in which the ancient interest of the race in religion seems unnecessary to a newly won competence and security.

Virginia Woolf, in her recent book *A Room of One's Own*, has described vividly the effects on her mind and her whole outlook on life of receiving a legacy of five hundred pounds from her aunt: "Indeed, it is remarkable what a change in temper a fixed income will bring about. No force in the world can take from me my five hundred pounds. Food, house, and clothing are mine forever. Therefore, not merely do effort and labor cease, but also hatred and bitterness. I do not hate any man; he cannot hurt me. I need not flatter any man, he has nothing to give me. . . . Indeed, my aunt's legacy unveiled the sky to me, and substituted for the large and imposing figure of a gentleman, which Milton recommended for my perpetual adoration, a view of the open sky."

She has rather exactly described the sense of sufficiency and security which science has brought to a large number of people. Indeed, in some respects to our whole age science is the rich uncle who has left us a legacy. It seems more than sufficient for all our needs. Consequently, what Virginia Woolf calls the "imposing gentleman" recommended by Milton—in other words, God—can be left out of the picture.

Here, then, are the family heirlooms. The tense scene in hundreds of old-fashioned novels was that of the reading of the Will. There in the parlor, with the shades half drawn as a decent tribute to grief, were gathered the family and relations, fidgety with anxiety, in a mood in which were mixed a subdued sense of bereavement, apprehension, and hope. The lawyer at the table begins the fateful reading. Such a scene may well sum up our present thought. Here is the Will of the spiritual ancestors of the America of to-day. To us of the twentieth century the Puritan speaks: "I leave a sense of God; of responsibility to God; a tradition of duty and the high seriousness of life. I leave an inheritance of devotion to the human rights of the individual and their expression in democracy. To you also I leave, with all the conflict involved, an exaltation of material success; a sanctification of profit; a strong momentum to the acquisitive instinct which sadly belies my affirmation that the chief end of man is to 'glorify God and to enjoy him forever.' "

The Pioneer hands on his legacy: "I bequeath a wilderness subdued and conquered for civilization; a new proving ground for a new order of life. I leave you stalwart elements of social strength and a happy valiancy, a tempered fortitude and hopefulness. To you also I leave an aggressive and undisciplined individualism; a preoccupation with material things, a religion of "getting on." With the ironical result that, having made civilization out of the wilderness, you may now struggle with forces which threaten to make a wilderness out of civilization."

The Machine speaks: "I give you a magical fairyland of mechanical progress, but a fairyland peopled with ogres and demons. I leave you a new freedom from drudgery and a new slavery of spirit; I leave you large comforts and moral mediocrity. I leave you external riches and internal penury, giant powers and pigmy purposes. And may God have mercy on your soul!"

But these are not the only figures who speak! Over the centuries comes the voice of a Young Man. He lived in a far distant age of remoteness from modern life, in an obscure province of the Roman Empire. He died in material bankruptcy. Yet he leaves to this day a measureless inheritance, a legacy which made one of his earliest followers cry out in exaltation, "We have the mind of Christ." That also is part of our national inheritance. Our problem to-day is to fuse the highest elements which come to us from Jesus with those which come to us from the development of life and character in our own nation and to dominate the unethical forces in our life and environment.

In 1836 Harriet Martineau made an appeal to the American people to "cherish the high democratic hope and faith in men. The older they grow," she says, "they must reverence the dreams of their youth." Part of our problem is nothing less than working out some original American social ideals with the momentum of a Christian faith.

The new State Capitol building of Nebraska is a striking symbol of the American hope. Its wide base in the form of a rectangle two stories high, typifies the widespread, fertile Nebraska plains. The central tower, serving as the chief architectural feature of the building, and rising triumphantly to a height of four hundred feet, expresses the aspiration and ideals of the citizens reaching upward to the highest and noblest in civilization.

The Capitol forms a monument not only "to the outdoor life of the agricultural State, but also of the aspiration of the pioneer community which broke its hard soils in order to provide a basis for a more splendid cultural future." Here, then, is pictured the goal—to rear on the base of a horizontal civilization, broad in its domain and achievement, a vertical civilization whose upward reaching ideals and standards will dominate and give meaning to the whole.

CHAPTER V

EXTERNALISM

In 1876 the United States gave a birthday party —the Centennial Exposition at Philadelphia, marking a hundred years of independence. The feature of that exposition which attracted the most popular attention was a large Corliss engine enthroned in the center of Machinery Hall. It was a tremendous affair, set up like a graven image of heroic size made of steel and brass. The revolving of its enormous flywheel generated one thousand six hundred horse power and made the whole building quiver and throb. There was a high fitness in placing the engine on the central throne of the exhibition. Nothing could serve quite so well as the symbol of two centuries of the machine, although no one realized then the extent to which the machine would make the second century a contrast to the first. For just as that engine at the Centennial set the building into a rhythmic throb, so the forces which the machine put in motion in the next fifty years brought a new tempo into the life of a people. The industrialism and the commerce which rose on the base of the machine have not only made a thoroughgoing transformation in the outward environment of life, but in the inner character, the social habits and the prevalent mentality of the population as well. With some degree of truth, indeed, the result could be called an industrial twentieth-century parallel to the old Genesis story of creation. God made man out of the dust of the ground in his own image. The machine is making man from the steel filings of the factory floor into its own image.

An order of life has been called into being which vastly complicates the task of creating a civilization which in any sense deserves the name "Christian." To say this does not mean that all the characteristic forces of the industrial age are pulling against Christian ideals. It certainly does not mean that a Christian order is an impossible goal. But these forces have vastly complicated the task. New and complex problems have been brought into human relationships. These relationships have been made so impersonal, involved in such a complicated network, that often their anti-Christian and unethical character has been obscured and disguised.

There was a fitness in the machine occupying the center of the stage at Philadelphia in 1876 for the additional reason that it was the engine's birthday as well as that of the nation. The year 1776 was marked not only by the Declaration of Independence, but also by the first successful use of the steam engine. These two events occurring in the same year have frequently been cited as a striking piece of irony: proclamation of independence and the instrument of a new slavery appearing at the same moment on the human stage. That there is irony in it cannot be denied. This has called forth the familiar picture of our being the slaves of the machine instead of its masters. Much has been made of the scene to be witnessed in a modern automobile factory, where the pressroom workers are handcuffed to the machine they operate. That manacling is done to prevent their being injured.

Nevertheless, it lends itself readily as a sort of crude symbolism of the new slavery to the machine which is characteristic of the second century of independence. This idea of the new slavery offers a fine chance for ranting, and the opportunity has been much improved. Listen to the high, shrill protest against the machine and all its works—it is the voice of Oswald Spengler—and it may well serve as a symbol of a thousand cries of "Woe unto me!"

Man has felt the machine to be devilish, and rightly. . . . There will come a time when he will blot the whole thing from his memory and his environment, and create about himself a wholly new world, in which nothing of this devil's technique is left.

Much of this protest is as futile as Ruskin's journey across England in a coach as a protest against the steam railways, or, to go back farther for a parallel, as the famous rebuke reported to have been delivered by King Canute to the impertinent waves advancing around the base of his throne on the sands.

Such protests leave two things out of the picture. They fail to recognize the measureless service which the machine has rendered to human welfare, the lifting of burdens from the shoulders of millions, widening the range of satisfactions, adding to the comfort, convenience, and dignity of life. It has been estimated that there are three billion mechanical slaves in America, thirty servants for every man, woman, and child. It would be a blind extravagance to pretend that all these servants have become masters. A crucial mistake of many bitter protesters is in ascribing the ills of our present order to the machine itself rather than to the real cause—the business system which operates the machine. Following the distinction made by Veblen, industry with its scientific and industrial processes is one thing; industrialism which directs and exploits them, is another.

The threat to human welfare and personality is undoubtedly present in industry. Its possible assault on personality is vividly pictured by Mr. Arthur Pound:

America gave the automatic tool its chance. Its blessings are evident, but, unless controlled by social conscience, it may develop curses equally potent, . . . undirected, it may push the human race into a new slavery, or stampede it into a new anarchy. . . . So far as the great majority of the workers are concerned, modern industry presents this phenomenon—the dulling of the mind—on a scale unequaled in extent, and to a degree unequaled in intensity, by anything on record in history. . . . Our tenders of machines are being starved in their souls.

But very often it is overlooked that the damage to human life does not come from power in industry or the utilization of power in industry; it comes, rather, from the greed-driven organization which manipulates power. It is the elevation of wealth as a goal of human effort rather than the mechanism which wealth controls, which makes the unethical character of much of our civilization. The machine is made to serve as a scapegoat for guilt that reaches higher up. Brutal exploitation did not come into the world with the machine, nor is it a necessary accompaniment of the machine age. There have been many occasions long before the dawn of the industrial revolution, before a steam whistle had ever blown

or a tool been harnessed to a motor, such as a
Roman galley ship, for instance, where perfect hell
had been created for dehumanized workers by the
operation of soulless exploitation.

Nevertheless, the machine may well stand as the
symbol of the forces which have created new problems and evolved some traits dominant at the present time in the American people. With this distinction in mind, between the applied science of
industry and the business system which controls it,
let us look at some of the chief traits which the combination of the two is fostering. Let us begin with
one of the most apparent and obvious results of
an age of mass production—its piling up of an unprecedented profusion of things. When we take
into our imagination even the most general picture
of the mountains of goods by which we are surrounded, there is small wonder that many observers
find a principal mental trait of America to be
"externalism." Merely to live, and move, and have
our being in the greatest warehouse of manufactured
goods the world has ever seen would develop that
quality.

John Dewey on his seventieth birthday anniversary dinner in November, 1929, said that in his
opinion externalism was the chief mark of the
American people to-day. By externalism, we mean
preoccupation with the material surface and instruments of life, which comes partly from the emphasis
of the practical which is part of the primary heritage,
partly from the lavish production of the machine,
from the drive of capitalism and the multiplication
of wants which at the present time is unquestionably
the greatest of American industries. We may re-

write our Stevenson, "The world is so full of a number of things, I am sure we should all watch out lest they cave in on us and smother us." There is such a profusion of things in the foreground that the mind becomes like a photographic plate on which twelve different exposures have been taken. Life is like a parade before a series of brilliantly lighted store windows all full of goods screaming for attention. Statisticians have calculated that one hundred years ago the average person had just about 72 wants, of these 16 being regarded as necessities; to-day the average person is, by the same calculators, said to have 484 wants of which 94 are rated as necessities. More than that, a century ago there were not more than 200 different items urged on the average man by the seller; to-day there are something like 32,000.

The total number of items sold in the United States to-day including different brands of one type of article, is about 365,000. This is a natural result of an age and a country in which for the first time material comfort is within the reach of all. We should not overlook all which that means for human welfare. Comfort for millions of people and the standard of living have enormously improved. But on the obverse side, like the dyer's hand, the soul has become subdued to what it works in. The external instruments and the processes based on them have invaded the mind and character.

A historical picture of the sharp conflict brought about by this mood of externalism is found in the Gospels in the story of the day of the triumphal entry of Jesus into Jerusalem. Jesus and the disciples are walking about the city. The disciples are awe-struck by the scene. "Look, Master!" they cried, "look at the buildings, look how big they are." It was, no doubt, a natural feeling of curiosity and interest on the part of countrymen unused to the city. Perhaps some of them were making their first visit to their country's capital. Yet, the words express a vivid contrast between the mind of Jesus brooding on the spiritual significance of the events which had taken place and the disciples' mind absorbed in externals. "Look! Look!"—that is the watchword of our time,—"look at the buildings, look at the houses, look at the automobiles, look!" That mood is as antagonistic to Jesus' conception of life and its values as was the mood of the disciples on the first Palm Sunday.

This preoccupation has been well expressed by a European observer, who confessed that in our country he had "a sense of everything being in a show window with nothing behind." Not long ago in New York City there was an accident in a building occupied by a Five and Ten Cent store. The floor caved in and a perfect avalanche of jimcracks rained down on the people beneath. There were no fatal results beyond being almost buried in the flood of things. This accident may well stand for what has actually happened in the lives of multitudes. They have been caught in a swirl of things which has come down on them with the result that the inner life has been flattened out. The table of contents of a million minds would just about be exhausted with some such entries as these—apartments, balloon tires, baseball, radios, five-cent cigars, installment–buying, vacuum cleaners, electric refrigerators, tabloids, talkies, overstuffed furniture, sun porches,

body squeaks.   There is no place for the soul, even
in the index.   Mr. Charles Merz has drawn a vivid
picture of this Sunday afternoon absorption in the
external scene:

Horns toot. Out on the road of pop-stands, gas tanks,
water-cans, hot dogs, ukeleles, kewpie dolls, and choco-
late almond bars that is now the highway of a nation,
one car slips past the slow-mover who is holding up the
line. Another car. A third, a fourth, a fifth, a sixth.
The pace picks up again. Twilight in September. Over
the hills winds the caravan: looking for something, nothing, everything. Lunches gone, lights twinkling, tonneaus
full of golden-rod, America revisited.

Somewhere a slow-mover is holding up the line. He
creeps along, deaf, dumb and blind; rebellion in his rear.
More sirens blare; clutches shift; brakes bite. What is
the matter up there, anyhow? Somebody must be looking at the scenery! Doesn't that fellow know that if the
rest of us don't get to Jamesport at 2:30 we won't reach
Creston until after three?—and if we don't reach Creston
until after three?—well, then we won't reach Smithtown
by 3:45. . . . Not that there is anything special for us
to do at Smithtown.

A generation ago it was very common to find a
book on the center of nearly every parlor table.
Certainly, throughout the small cities and towns,
and open country, that book was the Bible.   To-day
in many of these homes you can still find a book on
the center table, but it is not the Bible.   It is a
mail-order house catalogue.   And that substitution
of one book for the other is a mute testimonial to
this mood of externalism.

Citizens of the United States may ride on rubber
tires over concrete highways from coast to coast,

they snatch music from the air, they can see a world unrolled before their eyes, they are upholstered in security and comfort. Yet their souls may be too fat to yearn for anything.

We have learned an intricate and extensive conjugation of the verb "to have"; we have not done so much with the greater verb "to be." We live in a world in which "having" has gone beyond the wildest dreams, but a world in which "being" is to be classed as among the lost arts.

The intellect is primarily, sometimes almost exclusively, adapted to the needs and conditions of the external world. A natural result is that since externals make up a large part of experience, there is a continual need for new stimuli. It has been observed, consequently, that "behaviorism," the interpretation of the physical and mental life of man entirely in terms of reaction to physical stimuli, is a natural product of America. Such interpreters say that the average American's life is made up so largely of external stimuli that the condition inevitably gave rise to a philosophy which embodied it.

This absorption with the mechanisms or upholsteries of life reveals itself strikingly in the home. "Simplicity," says Mr. J. A. Spender, "and thrift, the art of making a little go a long way, the cultivation of the fireside, have few votaries." In the same strain Santayana writes, "To be poor in order to be simple, to produce less in order that the product may be more choice and beautiful, and we may be less burdened with ordinary duties and useless possessions—that is an ideal not yet articulate in the American mind." The formation of public opinion is not so much the result, as is so often stressed, of

the direct force of large financial powers, as of the
pervasive influence of the mentality of multitudes
who find their happiness in things and who make
things the center and circumference of life.   The
characteristic American tragedy of the inner life is
not the tragedy of Blue Beard, it is not that of the
man who has locked away in his breast some shameful secret which cannot bear the gaze of the world;
it is, rather, the far more subtle tragedy of Mother
Hubbard—nothing there!   When material luxuries
become necessities the converse is true, with all its
consequences, that spiritual necessities become un-
attainable luxuries.   This was one of the sure in-
sights of Thoreau, when he records the discovery
that people are so eager to get the ostentatious
necessities of a civil life that they lose the opportunity
to profit by civilization itself; while their physical
wants are complicated, their lives culturally are not
enriched in proportion, but pauperized and bleached.
Porcelain bath tubs are so much easier to obtain
than peace of mind; the thrill of speed is so much
more obvious than the "splendor of a sudden
thought," the peace of economic security, which all
can understand, is so much more tangible than the
peace of God which passeth understanding, that
we readily lose life in absorption with its machineries.

When we turn from this great feast for the eye
and all the senses to the Sermon on the Mount with
its emphasis on the supremacy of the life of the spirit,
its appeal for concentration upon that life, we see a
conception of life to which our present national
obsession is opposed at almost every point.   What
Jesus taught was not sterile introspection, but the
supremacy of the inner life.   Jesus' teaching might

be pictured in the words, "My mind to me a kingdom is"—a kingdom maintained against the anarchy of a clutter of outward things. Life grows mean when its history can be told largely in terms of things which happen outside of the mind and spirit. The religion of Jesus makes as its supreme demand that the human spirit *be* something, not merely have something. The mood of externalism prevents that inner achievement which Henry N. Wieman calls in a fine phrase, "the greatest collective artistry in the world, the art of reshaping the total process of living."

The first step leading out of the desert of externalism is to recognize the antagonism it presents to the mind of Jesus. Over a wide area there is only the faintest kind of recognition of the deadly ravages of that preoccupation with the externals of life. The good seed of the Kingdom is choked with weeds; finding no place in our crowded soil, it withers and droops. Instead of that conflict being recognized, the Christian ideal of the primacy of the life of the spirit is frequently conceived as something unrelated to actual life—a sort of pastoral painting, like a beautiful and delicate Corot hung on the walls of an overcrowded warehouse. A friend of Whistler's once called on the artist to advise him concerning the hanging of a painting which had been purchased a short time before in Paris. He complained to Whistler that he could not seem to make the painting fit the room. "Man," said Whistler, "you're beginning at the wrong end. You can't make that painting fit the room. You will have to make the room fit the painting." It is just as pertinent a truth in regard to Christian living. We have been trying to make Jesus' emphasis on the life of the spirit fit into the crowded room in which we live instead of rearranging our room to fit his picture of life.   There is a sort of quaint ring to-day to the old phrase "saving souls."   That phrase has been warped and pressed into the most mechanical molds. But there is a real high and timeless meaning in the words "saving a soul."   The real significance of life is never to be found in an external parade.   It is in an internal drama.   Seeking to maintain an American standard of living must be subordinated to holding a Christian standard of life.

It is not a hopeless matter.   Many have mistaken a temporary condition for a permanent one, as though it were set in concrete.   Strong forces of the human spirit are at work making for a revaluation of our life.   One of these is the inability to find happiness in things.   There has been the growing realization, by many, of the thinness and superficiality of much American life, when the all-dominating object has been to find happiness in things, a childish delight in luxuries, in contrivances, speed, and bigness.   For a picture of this failure, carefully done with a thousand details, turn to *Middletown*, by Robert S. and Helen Lynd.   One reader has summed up the effect of that picture thus: "The beauty that was the wilderness and the spirit that was the pioneer have become the thing-full emptiness of a mid-western town."   The emergence of an allied spiritual force in our midst has been eloquently expressed by Irwin Edman: "There has certainly never been a time or a place where, if delight or salvation were to be found in things, it should more emphatically be present than in the United States

at present. But a great many people are discovering the fact, not unknown to the Greeks or to
Thomas Aquinas, that felicity or deliverance is not
there to be found. So out of a weariness of things
there is a turn in many quarters to something as far
away from things as may be, to mystical moments
of insight, where things become either irrelevant or
incredibly enriched with meaning, to pauses of contemplation or of ecstasy where the letter no longer
killeth and the spirit may once again live."

But until the church sees the threat to a Christian
life which exists in our tendency to externalism it
can never make alliance with that ally.

A special form of externalism is the worship of
bigness. The kindest and shrewdest of all our
critics, James Bryce, in the first edition of his
American Commonwealth, singles out as one of the
most obvious marks of American mentality a
tendency to confuse bigness with greatness.

That tendency has certainly not been lessened
in the thirty-five years since Bryce made the judgment. The worship of size has been a growing
mark of an America in which the size of things becomes constantly larger. "Growth," Sinclair Lewis
declares, "is now the chief American ideal." Just
growth. "Watch Jonesville Grow" is a slogan for
every Jonesville and all the Joneses who live there.
G. W. Steevens, the English journalist, in his book
The Land of the Dollar, records a little incident which
throws up this trait into a strong light. He quotes
the words of a man about to show off his creamery.
" 'I am now about to show you my creamery. It
is not yet finished, but when it is, I anticipate that it
will be the most complete and best appointed'—

I shuddered, for I knew instinctively what was coming— 'in the world.' Would I ever escape the
tyranny of the biggest thing in the world!"

The tyranny of bigness—that is a persistent form
of autocracy against which the Declaration of Independence does not avail, but against which a new
national declaration of independence is desperately
needed. Lewis Mumford traces the beginning of
the trait to colonial days when in a time of small
things qualitatively people took refuge in quantity.
Hence arises, he says, our widespread feeling that a
thing becomes a hundred times as important if it is
a hundred times as big. We "lisp in numbers for the
numbers come." For most Americans the real tables
of the law and the gospel as well are the multiplication tables. Statistics are substituted for values, a
habit increased materially in an industrial and
scientific age which rests so heavily on measurement.

Respect for quantity, size as an end in itself, has
become a sort of religion—a powerful religion. It
has its ritual of crossing oneself in the presence of the
biggest, a blind devotion to mere increase, a loyal
refraining from questioning the value of a thing or an
institution, if only it be big. The city with the
greatest population, the store with the largest sales,
the motion-picture actor with the biggest salary—
to us these are objects of awe. This is due in part
to a prevalent adolescent mentality and in part to
the ascendency of a business philosophy. It is the
flower of a money culture, for bigness means profit.
This is the explanation to the blind passion for growth
seen in our cities. A traveler in Detroit hearing a
great deal of the phrase "Greater Detroit" asked three
residents of the city with whom he happened to be

lunching just what the phrase meant. None of
them could give an exact answer. One of them
thought that it meant the determination to have a
bigger population than the city now had. Another
said that it meant "greater than Cleveland." The
third had the true faith in him. He said it meant
"greater than Chicago." Thus there is the pell-
mell rush of cities to expand just at the time when
the largest cities are breaking down in many of
their fundamental services, such as transportation,
through sheer mass.

To confuse the size of anything with its significance is the most fundamental vulgarity of which
anyone can be guilty. Greatness is always more and
other than bigness. As long as that confusion
prevails widely, the common phrase "American vulgarity" will have a real meaning. As long as that
confusion prevails there will be a fundamental
antagonism to Jesus' whole scale of values. To
Jesus the significance of life is always to be measured
by quality, not by quantity. Not the size of cities
but the kind of life lived in them; not the mountains
of manufactured goods but the kind of men created
in the process; not bank clearing but abundant life—
that is the way Jesus reads the human balance sheet.
An alarming thing is the extent to which quantitative
measurement has invaded the church; the degree to
which it has been infected with the very vulgarity
it should combat. Statistical measurement of the
institution rather than the ethical transformation of
the life about it, is the standard which churches
frequently apply. Ask a company of church
people about the progress of religion and eight times
out of ten you will get an answer in statistical

terms. The adding machine displaces the cross on the altar.

There is nothing more needed than for the church to recover for itself, where it has been lost, Jesus' emphasis on ethical and spiritual quality, and to carry that over into life. Only such a domination of the quality of life over quantity of material will enable a nation to overtake its real purpose. Salvador de Madriaga has put this old truth in moving words within the last few months:

The pride of a nation should be in the number and quality of the choice individuals she produces; in her capacity for evolving such an environment that human beings should blossom out in her midst as flowers in a well-kept garden. Since every nation has her own distinctive natural conditions of race and soil, this ideal is bound to lead to the clearest development of nationhood and to the truest enrichment of life.

Such an ideal implies a scale of values wholly at variance with that which a purely statistical or economic conception of life implies. When we have proved that a particular course of action is economically "sound" we have not established that it is desirable. What is our ultimate aim?

If our standards are statistical, if our ambition for our nation is that it should produce more goods for more people, there is nothing more to be said. But if our standard consists in seeing the measure concerned does not interfere with the amenities of the garden in which our human beings are flourishing, in guaranteeing that our economic growth is not going to cripple men and women spiritually, then we must submit the proposal to a more thorough scrutiny than that of our economists.

The most thoroughgoing and redeeming scrutiny is that of the searching eyes of Jesus.

3

Partly from this subordination of value to magnitude comes one result characteristic of many aspects of American activity—an absorption in processes rather than a consideration of ends. There is an interest in mechanization as an end in itself which obscures the results of that mechanization in human life. The result is that the processes and mechanics of life are often so much more marvelous than the uses to which they are put. H. G. Wells says that "science is like a rich uncle who is crowding up the children with too many toys which they do not know how to use." It is a picture which illustrates one of the most penetrating judgments of Jesus— "What shall it profit a man to gain the whole world and lose his own life?" In our day we may ask the question, What shall it profit a civilization to gain a whole world of processes, a universe of whirling wheels and manufactured goods, and lose its real life? It is the irony of life being swallowed up by its accessories. It is the inherent danger of a complex age that as the outside grows more and more ingenious and imposing, the inside grows flat.

Macaulay in his essay on Milton laid down with stately march of rhetoric the thesis that, "As science advances, poetry inevitably declines." We might defend a similar thesis for our day—that as the aids to life multiply, life itself has a tendency to dwindle. The aids to life so readily become substitutes for it. Very characteristic of this mechanization becoming an end in itself is the story of the manufacturer who installed in his plant an elaborate and ingenious filing system. A month after the installation the salesman who had sold it called on the manufacturer and asked how the filing

system was working. "Splendid," said the manufacturer; "better than we had hoped."

"That's fine," eagerly responded the salesman,
"and how is business?"

"Oh," was the answer, "we have had to give up
business in order to look after the filing system."

It is often the case that the business of living
becomes subordinated to attending the mechanism
by which it is supported. It is often true in education. Some schools have given up education in
order to keep the educational system going. There
are many places in our public-school system where it
is difficult to find a teacher who has any time for the
quaint, old-fashioned, menial task of actually teaching a pupil anything; they are all too busy giving
tests. They are too busy measuring intelligence
to have any time left for developing some intelligence
which might be worth measuring after awhile. So
churches have frequently given up religion in order to
keep the ecclesiastical system going. It was the
comment of a foreign traveler in America that as
soon as Americans get an idea they immediately
form a committee, and by the time the typewriters
get to clicking and the secretaries are engaged in
sending out letters they begin to wonder what the
original idea was.

There is a striking disproportion between the
greatness of man's inventions and the triviality of
the uses to which they are frequently put. This is
particularly true of the latest wonder which science
has put into man's hands—the radio. Sometimes
we get a glimpse of the possible service of the radio
to life's highest values, as in the broadcast of the
opening session of the London Conference on Dis-

armament, or of great music. But more frequently there is a stronger impression of the contrast between the wonder of the process and the inanity of the message going over the air. Thoreau made a similar observation many years ago when the first Atlantic cable was laid. To someone exclaiming over the marvel of it, Thoreau said, "Yes, it is wonderful. Probably the first news that comes over it will be that Princess Adelaide has the whooping cough." Anyone who has listened to dreary hours of advertising ballyhoo over the radio will feel the force of Thoreau's statement that "we have improved means to unimproved ends." Speaking of this aspect of the radio, Mr. Chesterton observed that "it is rather remarkable that the most amazing means of communication should have been developed at the precise moment in history when nobody had anything to say."

A few years ago there was arranged the most extensive radio hook-up ever achieved up to that time, by which twenty-five or thirty million people were brought within the range of one human voice. And all of it was put to the service of broadcasting the blows of a mauling exhibition that would have done credit to the Stone Age. We harness Niagara and use part of the power to illuminate a jiggling advertisement of chewing gum—an irritation to the eye and mind. We send men up in aeroplanes to perform prodigies of aerial navigation, only to disfigure the sky with the name of a cigarette. In New York city a few years ago there was dedicated an eight million-dollar moving-picture palace, and during the first week it served as a frame for the most inane twaddle that ever trickled out of Hollywood. It was an eight-million-dollar frame for a thirty-cent chromo!

It is the symbol or a whole order in which the material frame subordinates the picture, the culture, the character. That inevitably happens when mere mechanization becomes an end in itself.

This ironical result applies peculiarly to one aspect of mechanization—the production of speed. Much European comment on speed in America, like many other comments, is considerably overdone. The rate at which most railroad trains are run in the United States is an expression of ample and gracious leisure compared to the trains of England and France. But there is justice in the observation that a large part of mechanical science and skill in the United States has been channeled into the production of speed. It is an empty gain, so far as the cultural and ethical values are concerned. The attainment of speed tends to become an obsession, childishly elevated to an end in itself, a destructive force to real human values. One essential and inescapable fact about speed is that it kills color. Things moving at a great rate turn gray. Life moving at a fast rate also turns gray, losing rich human color. We see one result of the speeding up of life in the relentless drive of much factory production, in which workers are geared to a high speed belt until they become what Edison calls the lower level of machine tenders—"semi-automatics." But they are "semi-automatics" with aching muscles and taut nerves, drained of vitality and ready for the junk pile at forty.

Another obvious element on the balance sheet of the speed mania is the heavy toll of accidents both in industry and outside, though, of course, a large part of the industrial accidents are not so much the sole result of speed as of profit-making. For by a conservative estimate half the accidents in industry are preventable.

Taking its tempo from the machine, our whole national life is characterized by haste. A baby's first glance, as his uncomprehending eyes look out of the hospital window, lights on whizzing motor cars in the street, and for most of his life he will be kept in a state of nervous tension by the spectacle of rapid movement about him. Aeroplanes, automobiles, railroads call the tune of life and we all jump to their rapid beat. Not least of the results of this straining for speed is the developed love of excitement, especially in the young. "Our whole civilization is pitched in a higher emotional key which requires shriller notes to startle the audience." The brutalization of toil, the waste of life in accidents, the accelerated craze for physical and mental stimulation, the thinness and superficiality of a mode of living of which the chief mark is movement are the most evident results of a passion for speed. These are directly in antagonism to ethical and spiritual values. Against them the wisest strategy does not lie in the negative process of trying to slow up, but in the larger positive task of so elevating human values to the first place that whatever denies and destroys them will be throttled down.

CHAPTER VI

THE RELIGION OF PROSPERITY

CLOSE together on some typewriters are two keys, one of them brought much more into use than the other, but both symbols of universal forces of the soul—the dollar sign and the exclamation point. Perhaps there is real significance in the fact that many typewriters do not have an exclamation point; it is unthinkable that one should be made without a dollar sign. The forces which we have been considering so far—externalism, the worship of size, mechanization, and speed—may be represented by the exclamation point, the amazement at the material progress of the modern world. There is no question, however, but that the influence symbolized by the dollar sign is more continuous, pervasive, and powerful in our life. The situation may be represented by an equation between the terms $\$ = !$. The dollar sign has become our most ecstatic exclamation point. It has gathered to itself over a large area of life the moods and attitudes usually associated with religion. It calls forth awe, aspiration, loyalty, and service. John Dewey puts this clearly in his statement that the central fact of our civilization is that we are living in a money culture.

To say this is by no means to subscribe uncritically and blindly to the common, shopworn indictment of the United States as a materialistic nation, the land of the almighty dollar, driven by a passion for money-making which supposedly surpasses that of

any other people.   Like all stereotypes, that generalization is far too simple to fit the facts.   It is the
kind of thing which results from a "tea tour of the
United States."   Its most complete refutation has
come not from the retorts of angered Americans but
from acute and capable foreign critics.   Again and
again this has been shown to be a surface generalization.   The extent of generosity and charity,
the benefactions which are so obvious a mark of
America, indicate much indifference to money in itself.   The city editor of any newspaper will always ad-
judge the discovery of a miser, a real specimen of the
type so dear to melodrama, to be front-page news.
The charge of materialism is particularly interesting
when it comes, as it often does, from France.   The
members of the A. E. F. acquired considerable data
on that subject in the course of their adventure.
The classic literature of money grasping is not to be
found in the work of any American or anyone writing
of America; it is to be found in Balzac.   The panorama of the *Comédie Humaine* pictures an intense
passion for acquiring and clutching money, which
is quite foreign to America.   The scraping for a
dowry, the goal of security, amassing of funds
sufficient to retire on show a concern for money in
itself not to be matched on this side of the Atlantic.
Early in the century the Frenchman Chevalier wrote
of life in the United States, "Nowhere do you see
specimens of that sort of avarice of which examples
are so common among us."

It is not the primacy of avarice, but the unchallenged ascendency of business as the absorbing game
which is the leading feature of the American scene.
Hugo Münsterberg shows this in a lively figure:

"The American chases after money with all his mind exactly as on the tennis court. He tries to hit the ball, and it is the game he likes and not the prize. If he loses, he does not feel as if he had lost a part of himself, but only as if he had lost the last set in a tournament." It is true this is far too generous a compliment. The prize bulks much larger than in Münsterberg's estimate. But the zest, the thrill of conflict and conquest which in other nations spread out into more different fields of life are in America channeled more narrowly and exclusively into business. Lewis Mumford put this interpretation into compact, and perhaps extreme, form, "In America industry was not merely bread and butter; it was love, adventure, worship, art, and every sort of ideality." Here was this field "we have chosen for high adventure." Just as in the spacious days of the great Elizabeth sea dogs like Hawkins and Drake ranged the sea in quest of prizes, so in the more spacious days of Henry Ford adventurers ranged the field of factory, clearing house, and stock market. Dollars or doubloons— it is the same game for the same prize.

This domination by the business mind has been partly due to the fact that business is and has been the only field in which high and exclusive position and social prestige could be won. This has long been recognized, but has never been more effectively stated than by James Truslow Adams in his book "*Our Business Civilization*," in which he has summed up in compact form the influences which have caused the shaping of the whole pattern of American life and business interests. The fact that in America there was a soil to exploit profitably beyond the dreams of European peoples, no hereditary nobility, the abolition of social distinctions, no strong tradition giving to the professions a rival or superior place to business—all these opened the way for the domination of business ideals. America has no honors list except the tax list. To that fact is often given the credit for the great habit of joining, for the flourishing of fraternity orders—the Elks, the Moose, the Beaver, and Busy Bee, all the animals in the menagerie. But far more important for the ascendency which it gives to economic success is the elevation of the profit motive to the first place as the national orthodoxy. "America," says Waldo Frank, "took the fragmented authority of Europe and set it squarely on the brow of possession." Henrik Van Loon, in his *Story of America*, has a striking drawing of a group of skyscrapers on the lower tip of Manhattan Island, in which all stand like the leaning tower of Pisa—a suggestion of a lopsided civilization. Certainly, the domination of economic success has made, and is making, a people lopsided in that the formation of such a large part of our mind is under the play of one interest.

Here is the crux of the battlefield. In this concentration on property is the strongest and sharpest clash between the American mind and the mind of Jesus. It is as Harry F. Ward has observed, the clash between "the ethic of Jesus, which tells us to love our neighbor, and the accepted rule of business which commands us to make a profit out of him."

Any discussion of business which would leave out of view its contribution to human welfare would be more lopsided than the leaning skyscrapers just mentioned. Those contributions are not stressed here, for they have occupied the spot light of attention. It is an unforgettable part of our rosary that we have in America the highest standard of living of any nation in the world and of any period of history. America has produced the greatest amount of comfort and luxuries for the largest number of people, though it must not be forgotten that the business system takes unctuous credit for what belongs chiefly to the prodigality of nature and scientific discovery. In many industries we find the highest standard of wages of any country at any time. In those achievements there are enormous human benefits. The old worn observation to the effect that the man on the street has comforts and conveniences which place him far above the kings and lords has profound truth in it. Unquestioned also is the fostering of certain real virtues, mostly the so-called economic virtues, such as honesty, industry, thrift, and sobriety. Beyond that, there has been a stimulation in varying degree of the social virtues of co-operation. The stress on the unethical consequences of business ascendency does not spring from blindness or from sentimentalism, but from a realistic sense of its warping of the individual character and personality, and its elevation of property values above human values. The keen vision and insight of Ralph Waldo Emerson before the first half of the nineteenth century had passed, pictured the ethical and spiritual liabilities of a civilization overwhelmingly dominated by commercialism: "A question which well deserves examination now is the danger of commerce. This invasion of nature by trade with its money, its

credits, its steam, its railroad, threatens to upset
the balance of man and to establish a new universal
monarchy more tyrannical than Babylon or Rome.
Very few or faint are the poets or men of God."

These words of Emerson find an echo in the words
of another New Englander seventy-five years later
when the processes foreseen by Emerson were well
along in their course. John J. Chapman said in 1928
with perhaps intentional exaggeration because he
was speaking at a dinner under the auspices of the
Harvard School of Business Administration, "The
United States is a mill which turns everything into
business—love, art, leisure, science, innocent recreation and religious contemplation are ground up
into business packages and marked as soon as
nature—prodigal, unabashed, procreant nature—
produces them."

What has happened is that the enormous reserves
of energy, partly the result of the pioneer development of a century and partly of later increment,
have been directed predominantly into the one
outlet of money-making, often with the relentless
and unremitting drive, accompanied by an equally
unremitting pace of the material enjoyment of
money. It is a development like that of the energy
drawn from the expansive area of the Great Lakes
being channeled into the narrow limits of the
Niagara River, with a similar result of driving force,
though emphatically not a spectacle of equal beauty.

The dominance of business is giving a new elevation to the profit motive as the mainspring of life,
just at the time that industry's use of science has
given powerful instruments to greed. A phrase
used a short while ago to the effect that business was

a game had a sort of playful sound to it, but within the game as it is played with masses of people as pawns, the observer realizes that it is often a game like a romp with a Bengal tiger. That the tiger has teeth and claws and is not held back from using them from sentimental restraints is only too evident. "The very men who give freely to public ends have driven their chariots over many industrial corpses."

The combination of business ascendency and scientific tools has been summed up by John Dewey in his statement that the basic fact of our American civilization is a high technology in the service of the profit motive. "There lies," he says, "the serious and fundamental defect of our civilization." This might be symbolized in one of the newest and most ingenious inventions which has recently been put into operation. This is an improvement of the stock ticker which by a new device is able to record approximately five hundred characters a minute in turning out the day's transactions on the Exchange floor. The machines formerly in service type only two hundred eighty-five characters a minute. At the top of the crash in October, 1929, when thirteen million shares were exchanged in a day, the ticker was two hundred and fifty-five minutes behind the margin. This new high-speed ticker is a perfect illustration of scientific ingenuity pressed into the service of large and quick profits.

When we consider the amazing mechanical achievements we cannot help being impressed with the thought of what they might mean to the abundant life for men—that all-inclusive purpose of Jesus. We have been repeatedly told by engineers that there is enough technical knowledge and skill now

at command which could lift the burdens which
have crushed mankind, abolish poverty, more than
double the standard of living and deliver men from
many of the scourges which have crippled and
blighted life. Surely, here are enough skill and
resources. Why is it not done? The answer is
simple. There is more immediate profit to be
made for some interests in the present waste and
inefficiency. These results are sacrificed to the idol
of economic gain. Such results would require planning arranged with general social welfare in view,
and that is not the primary aim. The immediate
aim of business must be, first of all, to make money.
If this seems like a too easy generalization, let us
get out of rhetoric into objective fact. Go through
the pages of *Middletown*, by Robert S. and Helen
Lynd. This book contains the facts of the most
painstaking and thorough objective study ever made
of a modern city. Here we find no trace whatever
of the disdain and contempt which have so freely
colored observations on American life. The writers
did not go to Middletown to prove anything, but to
examine the life of a representative American community. "Middletown" is the name given in the
book to an actual city in Indiana, Muncie, a town of
thirty-eight thousand people, chosen because of the
typical features which it shares with more than one
hundred other towns and cities of about the same
size. The population is largely composed of native
born, of native parentage. Prosperity has been
good to Middletown in the usual accepted sense of
prosperity. The material comforts which have
been so lavishly produced are there in abundance.
Two out of every three families own automobiles.

There are the usual features of the scene: Ten or a dozen motion picture theaters, the Chamber of Commerce, the usual luncheon clubs and the usual slogan which becomes a sacred creed that "Middletown is the best place on earth."

But when we look behind the surface, we find a majority of the population poorly housed, living on the border line of decent physical existence, if not under it. A considerable portion of the workers are haunted by the continual specter of unemployment; it is increasingly difficult for men over forty to fifty to find employment. When we look for other evidence of humane culture, we find business men reading considerably less than they did forty years ago; little or no discussion of intellectual or artistic matters. Here is a town in which money has been the chief measure of value; in which worth is assessed by money making. This tyranny results in a smug and narrow conservatism which controls social and political as well as business activities; in which almost all interest and thought of the purpose and meaning of life is crowded out. There is our real theme, when we consider the major forces which are making American character. For there we see the obdurate power of a community life organized on a money culture.

One aspect and result of this supremacy of economic gain in the United States to-day is the widespread speculation. For the past year since the stock crash in October, 1929, there has been a sober and chastened mood on stock gambling, though unquestionably this is more in the nature of remorse at being caught than a repentance induced by a vision of the unethical character of the opera-

tions. This desire to "make a killing" in the market
—even a mild and modest killing—is part of the
religion of prosperity; the risk involved is one of the
hazards of the faith. How much the increase of the
speculative habit is due to the hopeless feeling of
many that there is little chance of getting on finan-
cially through the ordinary rewards of labor, as James
Truslow Adams suggests, is hard to determine.
But of the spread of the fever there can be no doubt.
The invention just described—the speeding up of
the stock ticker—speaks of the growth and power of
this obsession with a staccato sharpness which cannot be muffled.

Just at the time that there has been among a
large number of the most thoughtful people of the
country, in the churches and outside, a growing
realization of the fundamental, unethical character
of gain without an equivalent return, comes this
wave of augmented passion to get something for
nothing. The conflict between our accepted ideals
and practice is shown by the feeling that while one
would scorn in private life to take a reward without
an equivalent return, it is "quite all right" in business.

George Bernard Shaw has defined a gentleman as
"one who tries to put back a little more than he takes
out." That is an essentially Christian attitude to
life. Yet nothing could be further from the prevailing philosophy of multitudes that the chief purpose of economic activity is to put in as little and
take out as much as you can.

We would see this conflict very clearly if we could
look into the mind of a man in church on Sunday
morning listening to the Scripture reading from the
Sermon on the Mount while thinking of the stock

market.   There the gap between a mind intent on
profit from manipulating the market and the central
ideas of Jesus is painfully evident. The two strands
weave together in his mind in something like this
confusion:

"Blessed are the poor in spirit for theirs is the
kingdom of — American Can gone up to 57. . . .
Blessed are the meek — that must mean the Amalgamated are really buying into it. . . . Blessed are
those that mourn—two hundred shares at ninety-
seven will come to. . . . Take no thought for the
morrow—I'll have to cover that drop in Con-
solidated Electric to-morrow or get caught short.
. . . But seek ye first the kingdom of heaven."

When we step out of that mind working in its
squirrel cage we feel that possibly Jesus may have
been right when he said, "No man can serve two
masters."

"Wall Street Branches Out"—thus runs the
familiar headline. The lure of quick profits by the
application of shrewdness and daring without any
social contribution beckons to millions. No wonder,
when prizes so glittering are dangled before their
eyes. Mr. Carl Snyder, of the Federal Reserve
Bank of New York, told the American Statistical
Association at its meeting in December, 1928, that
the number of millionaires in the United States has
increased from seven thousand in 1914 to more
than thirty thousand in 1928. He ascribes a considerable part of this increase to the enormous rise
in the value of securities since the Great War and
to the colossal manipulation in security values—
incomparably the greatest gamble the world has
ever known.

Stock exchange seats in New York are sold at almost six hundred per cent. increase over seven years ago. In 1895 there were only sixty-seven branches of the New York Stock Exchange outside of New York City; to-day there are well over one thousand.

This expanse has not been wholly due to the legitimate investor. In the past year or two, and to a predominant degree in the months before the crash, the gambler had routed the investor and pushed him to an inconsiderable place.

This increase of speculation has not been done mainly on savings but on millions of borrowed money which have hung a heavy weight on the credit system of the country, making a severe credit stringency. The traffic jam of gamblers has blocked the progress of legitimate business enterprises.

The extent and the spread of stock gambling is indicated in the columns of financial tips which appear every morning in the tabloid newspaper, the New York Daily News. Certainly, the News does not circulate chiefly among the moneyed classes. Here is one sample of the literature exposed to the millions every day:

Dupont is a corker; . . . there's at least 40 points in it if bought at the market. Stick with the Standards of N. Y. and N. J. . . . For a high-flyer Eastman Kodak can't be surpassed. . . . Natural Dairy Products are about ready to go. . . .

Buy Montgomery Ward and reap a substantial profit by Aug. 26. . . . The Market Goose hangs high as Broker's Loans dip. . . . U. S. Freight is to have a swirl upward. . . . The rails never looked better. . . . Don't go to bed to-night without having some American and Foreign Power in your strong box. . . .

For another picture done with conscious exaggeration and burlesque take George Creel writing in
Collier's Weekly:

An' now we've gone crazy over Wall Street gamblin'.
No matter where you go, the one subject of conversation
is melons, mergers, margins an' millions, with a low,
moanin' undertone about how everything goes up the
minute you sell it. If you happen to mention Art or
Literature, people give you a dirty look, or want to know
if they're on the Big Board or the Curb, where you got
the tip, an' what ought you to hold for.

Stocks, stocks, stocks!

My cook left yesterday because I wouldn't put a ticker
in the kitchen, my chauffeur doesn't report for duty until
the market closes, I have to read quotations to the gar-
bage man, an' the grocer boy came into my room at five
o'clock this morning, wantin' to know if the recent slump
meant the end of the bull market or was it only a technical readjustment an' corrective reaction.

Women are gamblin' jes' as insanely as the men. All
the big brokerage houses now provide parkin' space for
baby carriages, an' throw in a bottle of soothin' syrup
with every ten-share order.

Even this exaggeration is close enough to reality
to justify the hyperbole. A cartoon in the New
York World summed it up. It showed two babies
in their perambulators which had been parked together. One infant leaned over the side of his
carriage and remarked to the other, "I see Anaconda
has gone up two points."

Game manufacturers have capitalized the interest
in carrying over the speculative craze into games for
the home. The following is taken from an advertisement in the New York Times, April 7, 1929:

Ticker—the new Wall Street game that is sweeping America. Puts zip and spirit into every party. On the table is Wall Street complete—quotation board, ticket, stock certificates, margin calls, bear raids, extra dividends—the actual features of the Stock Exchange. You buy and sell stocks. They sky rocket or tumble. You are cleaned out or make your pile. Every session a riot. Teach it to the children.

Without any question the children are learning!

In this trend we get away from the basis on which human life has dignity and produces character; we get away from Jesus. Jesus did not say, "He that would be great among you let him cash in at the peak of the market." He said, "He that is greatest among you shall be your servant."

The point which must not be missed in all this is that this speculative fever is not fundamentally different from much of the motivation of business. It is just an outstanding instance which shows up the character of much of the whole.

The decorations of the many new office buildings convey suggestions quite other than and beyond any intended by the owners or architects. They are lofty skyscrapers—monuments to industry. Outwardly impressive, in the decorative scheme, in the windows, doorways, and general lines they are even more striking. It is done in ecclesiastical lines, giving one the impression of being in a massive cathedral. "This is not an office building," one exclaims; "this is a church! It is not a place of trade; it is a place of worship." Walking through the rotunda we seem to hear the echo of familiar words,

> "Storied windows, richly dight,
> Giving a dim, religious light."

The phrase used of it exactly describes it—a cathedral of commerce. In that phrase and in the churchly *motif* of the building itself is suggested one of the basic and far-reaching forces operating on American life—the extent to which a faith in prosperity and the economic creed and philosophy which are supposed to be the support of prosperity have taken on the characteristics of a religion. The office building in the guise of a cathedral gives visible form to a national orthodoxy.

In the use of such a figure of speech there is strong need to guard against a fantastic extravagance and misunderstanding. It is not meant to suggest that economic interest or success has displaced religion, or is in any formal sense at war against it. To anyone familiar with contemporary life that idea would be ludicrous. Nor does it mean to imply at all the acceptance of the stereotype, against which protest has been made earlier in these pages, of the United States as ruled by avarice. It does mean that the assumptions underlying the present economic order have a prestige and authority which reach into the lives and mind of men as a formative influence comparable to that of an accepted religion.

The justification for this comparison is all the more clear if we hold in mind William James' definition of a real religion as "the assumptions on which a man habitually acts." The assumptions basic to the ascendency of the present business order are those on which multitudes do habitually act. The prestige of that order and its acceptance keeps many from bringing those assumptions into examination in the light of their religious faith. Not that such examination is lacking. One of the most hopeful trends of our time is the scrutiny growing in extent and in realistic ruthlessness both from the stand-point of economic efficiency and social, ethical, and religious consequences of the present order.

It is no exaggeration to call these assumptions "an authoritative orthodoxy." Prosperity is both a morality and a religion. It has its high sanctities —that the very on-going of the business of the country depends on the acceptance of the profit motive as the only sufficient guarantee of the in-dividualistic drive necessary to industry; that what-ever is good for business is good for all; that the gain-ing of wealth is the chief end of man; that property rights precede human rights; that profit-making must never interfere with or at least must be very tenderly dealt with both by government and religion; that whatever disputes these dogmas is a blasphemy, a heresy to be stamped out.

One hundred years ago the Frenchman Saint Simon prophetically hailed the captain of industry as "the future priest of humanity." To a very real extent that prophecy has been fulfilled. The priests are now conducting regular services in the new cathedrals.

Like many expressions of Christianity the religion of prosperity is the religion of a Book. It has its infallible book—the Bank Book. Like many other religions in many places it is supported by force. It has its suppressions. Witness a Western city a few years ago in which the facts about an epidemic of infantile paralysis were kept suppressed, to the great risk to the health of the community, because broadcasting the facts would be bad for the tourist trade.

This religion has its missionaries full of apostolic zeal, who go about proclaiming that conditions in the United States are just about ninety-eight per cent right. The missing two per cent in the calculation is conclusive evidence of eminent fairmindedness!

The religion of prosperity has its commandments. It says, "Thou shalt have no other gods before me; for I the lord thy god am a jealous god." Bruce Barton sets forth the religious character of prosperity when he says in a syndicated editorial that "the greatest force for righteousness in the United States to-day is nothing less than business."

This religion has its inquisitions and excommunications. Witness the social, political, and even economic boycott in Massachusetts three years ago visited on those who vigorously asserted the belief that Sacco and Vanzetti were innocent. It was not a socialist orator declaiming from a soapbox, but Dean Willard L. Sperry, of the Harvard Theological School, who said, "It has been latterly professionally quite as dangerous for a Protestant minister to bolt the Republican party as to doubt the dogmas of his church." This is not to be wondered at. In many cases the dogmas of the party were the dogmas of the church.

In subtle, pervasive ways there is a parallel to William H. Seward's famous declaration, "There is a higher law than the Constitution." There is a higher law than Jesus, the profit motive proclaims, and it carries its point, not through open conviction, as much as through disguise. The most unabashed and complete expression of this dogma of the primacy of business has been expressed not by its critics, but by protagonists. What could be more perfect than the following from an editorial in "The Nation's Business" in December, 1927:

I can understand why a business man would admire Mussolini and his methods. They are essentially those of successful business. Executive action; deeds, not words. Executive action; not conferences and talk. Mistakes, yes, but action, a bit of the Jesuitical—the end justifies the means. A supreme contempt for red tape. Social control of factory, anathema. Material progress must precede spiritual, artistic and intellectual.

But if the religion of prosperity has this analogy to other religions, it has one more. There is a vigorous higher criticism at work—irreverent, irritating in its mastery of facts. It is chipping away to a dangerous extent at two of the pillars of economic orthodoxy. The first pillar is the dogma that capital and industrialism are responsible for the great mass of production and the resultant high standards of living, and, consequently, if that condition is to continue, to capital must go not only the lion's share of the profit but almost all of it. It is becoming ever more clear that the benefits which we now enjoy come more from inventions and from the prodigality of our national resources than from capital. Ownership is becoming more and more separated from operation, and instead of the drive for immediate profits being a help to industry it has saddled industry with waste and has blocked the beneficial results which the orderly minds of engineers might bring about.

The other pillar which is being chipped is the dogma that greed and possession are the only motives sufficient to supply the energy needed for the carrying on of economic life. More and more as the operation of other motives is seen, not only in other walks of life, but in the directing force of industry itself—in its technicians and administrators —that dogma is shown to be a cynical lie and a hoary blasphemy against human nature.

This religion of prosperity creates a mind-set in individuals antagonistic to the ethic of Jesus. Dr. Harry Emerson Fosdick has described how it has induced a browbeaten, inferiority complex from which people suffer. In a prosperity-minded popu-lation, not having much money, they either doubt themselves or allow themselves to be dominated by the hunger after prosperity. Another of its ravages is the extent to which the acceptance of economic success as the chief end of life harnesses to its service the sacred instinct of love. A young man may start out in life with idealistic aims which are pared down under the necessity to procure the material rewards of success as a prerequisite to establishing a home and family.

This dominance of business has spread into all fields. It is a commonplace that the corruption of politics is simply the extension of the profit motive into politics. The formidable difficulties in the way of all social welfare legislation are not in the main those connected with inertia and public igno-rance. The blocking of legislation looking to pre-venting the waste of material resources, the abolition of child labor, laws demanding safety devices, pro-tecting health, improving living conditions, en-forcing the pure-food enactment come from the economic interests affected. "Our whole capitalistic conception of business is to make money. And politics is just the business of politicians."

It was more than one hundred years ago that Wordsworth wrote these stinging lines concerning the corruption of politics in Pennsylvania:

"All who revere the memory of Penn,
  Grieve for the land in whose wild woods his name
  Was fondly grafted with a virtuous aim,
Renounced, abandoned by degenerate Men
  Have state-dishonor black as ever came
To upper air from Mammon's loathsome den."

The theme has remained timely for a century! These lines may have some application in the era of Grundy and Vare. Perhaps the most striking recent instance of the lust for profits reaching out to corrupt education was in the ingenious efforts of the light and power companies to poison the teaching in the public schools.

Let us look very briefly at a few of the results of the acceptance of the religion of prosperity to see what its sway means in terms of the life of millions.

Colonel W. A. Starrett, the head of one of the leading construction firms in the country, wrote two years ago the story of the skyscraper. He calls it "the most American thing in America." The life history of a skyscraper is a fascinating and amazing story—an incredible one to laymen, from the moment the engineers start calculating stresses to the time when ten or eleven different trades step on each other's toes in the finishing processes. At the close of the volume Colonel Starrett turns his attention to the human factors in the building, and the bright glitter of achievement changes into deep shadows. Three things are mentioned as the dark spots in the story of the skyscraper. The first is the number of strikes and labor conflicts. The second is the lowness of the wages, which are high by the day, but low by the year, coupled with the early end of the working period. The third dark shadow is the appalling loss of life. Steel erectors had two thousand accidental deaths in twenty years out of an average union membership of fifteen thousand men; that is, a man who worked steadily for the period had nearly one chance in seven of being killed on the job. If he survived, he found himself at the end of only twenty years worn out and no longer able to work.

A disturbing parable—this "most American thing in America." It pictures our glittering success in the mechanical achievement and our failure in human relations.

Step into the shadows which are cast on the face of men by the tower of industrialism.

One of the deepest is the impersonal character imparted to industry. It so often dehumanizes relations between men. They are separated by such long ranges that the eye does not focus on the men at the other end of the process. When the officials in an office in Chicago decide to lay off three hundred men in the branch factory five hundred miles away, the whole nexus is so impersonal that the human drama is never enacted before the eye. The same impersonal character applies to consumers as well as to employees. This is often blamed on the machine. Certainly, use of power machinery often results in making a man into a kind of mechanical tool as a mere part of a process. But, as has been said before, the blame laid on the machine itself belongs to the system and the motive which operates it. The driver is the most dan-

gerous part of any machine. Let greed be seated
at the lever and the impersonal character will be
brought out to the fullest extent. The fatalism
which accepts the status of the machine worker as
necessarily depersonalized is very superficial. It is a
status compelled by profit seeking rather than any
necessities of machinery. This treating of men as
means is the most direct antagonism to Jesus'
teaching of the sacredness of personality, of the
right of a man to be treated as an end in himself,
which can be imagined. How far that impersonal
character of industrialism has gone can be seen in
the attempt to set down in the background of the
mills of Pittsburgh or the textile mills of Marion,
North Carolina, the lines of the hymn, "Thine is the
loom, the forge, the mart." These words would
only be a mockery. Yet they express an ideal
which cannot be dropped from a Christian view of
the world.

Another broad shadow is that of insufficient liveli-
hood for multitudes of workers and their families.
It sounds like heresy to mention this when the
present call is so loud for the singing of hymns to
prosperity. If so, there are a good many heretics.
The fact that we have the highest standard of living
in general of any nation, at any time, and the additional fact of the operation of much industry on the
theory that high wages makes possible large consumption, are decidedly good. Nevertheless, the
fact remains that our prosperity is largely a luxury
prosperity, concentrated on a small proportion of the
population and most evident in the luxury trades;
it has not extended to such basic industries as textiles,
coal, and agriculture. It is still a fact that two

thirds of the families in the United States are now living beneath the line of the United States Department of Health's budget of decency.

Stuart Chase says that property has never been admitted in terms of the happiness and peace of mind, the wages and money income of over eighty per cent of Americans. The United States government reports that the average income for all persons gainfully employed in 1926 was $2,210. Yet ten thousand persons paid taxes on an income of ten thousand dollars a year and over, and two hundred twenty-eight paid taxes on incomes of over one million dollars and fourteen on incomes of over five million dollars. The National Bureau of Economic Research has computed that five per cent of the families of America get thirty per cent of the national income. What can be called prosperity is being enjoyed by the one fourth of the population which owns nearly all the property.

When we realize that one tenth of the population owns ninety-five per cent of the property, the use of the words "nearly all the property" are not rash. The average yearly wage for unskilled labor in the prosperous automobile industry for 1926 is given by the Employers' Association of Detroit at $1,200.

Allied with this shadow is the deep and growing one of unemployment, while profits pile up and melons are cut, without the protection of unemployment insurance or old-age security. Mr. Hoover, when Secretary of Commerce, said regarding this shadow, "There is, to my mind, no economic failure so terrible in its import as that of a country possessing a surplus of every necessity of life with numbers willing and anxious to work deprived of those ne-

cessities.   It simply cannot be if our moral and
economic system is to survive."

This most serious defect calls for money and
thought to be applied to its permanent conquest.
The very machines which have been lauded and
which have been the source of profits have thrown
men out of jobs on an unprecedented scale and the
rate of unemployment is constantly going up.   The
callous lack of responsibility is pictured by Mr. J.
A. Spender in his report of a conversation with
Henry Ford:

Mr. Ford seems genuinely pleased when I pay my
tribute to the works by smiling indulgently.   When I
hint at certain ruthless aspects of it, for instance, the
suspension for a year which had thrown so many workmen on their own resources, which friends in Detroit tell
me has meant for a good many of them on their beam
ends, he smiles indulgently. . . . These men have had a
good time and earned big wages for fifteen years; now
they must be patient until he was ready.   In life one
must have in mind the great objects and not let them be
thwarted by minor obstacles, else one would do nothing.
Then I talked about his interest in Americana.

Ah, yes, Americana!   The long lines of workless
men; the hundreds who lost their homes; those who
were thrown on the inadequate public charity of
Detroit; the suffering of women and little children—
these were not the sort of Americana which interested Mr. Ford that winter.   One must bear in
mind "great objects"!

The shadow of waste which the passion for profit-
making brings about falls heavily on people.   We
are not now speaking of the ruthless greed-driven
waste of material resources which coming genera-

tions will feel more keenly, but the waste which adds to the present burdens the population must carry.

This waste includes part of the enormous cost of distribution, the expense of advertising and selling often far exceeding the cost of actual manufacture, the frantic over-production and consequent unemployment and distress.

We have been looking at the major antagonisms to the Christian gospel and a few of the results. We are not blind to many strong evidences of a different spirit. Indeed, these new forces making for social responsibility and human feeling are the most hopeful movements of our day. Still, we must be on our guard against the danger of allowing even the finest evidences of a new feeling to blind us to the essential clash of Christian ethics to a greed-motivated system. In the blindness which causes Christian people to cry, "Peace, peace," when there is no peace, is the greatest danger.

The church as a whole must see, with far more clearness than it has yet done, that covetousness is a sin in the sense that murder and sexual immorality are sins. To get that clear vision in the mind of the Christian forces of the country is the primary and immediate task on which genuine progress waits.

Nathaniel Hawthorne once wrote down in his journal a suggestion for a possible story concerning a gas main underneath a city, which had a secret leak and gradually filled the whole city with its subtle poison. Hawthorne never wrote that story, but his germ idea of a broken gas main which filled the whole city with poison might well serve as a parable of a whole nation of cities. The poison gas in our national atmosphere is the exhalation from the ascendency of the profit motive, which, with the new powers which industrial and commercial development have given to acquisitiveness, steals like a subtle and blighting poison into every realm of life. That cannot go unchallenged if Christianity is to be anything more than a pious decoration on a pagan pattern of life. We cannot permanently have a Christian Church in a pagan society. Christianity must dominate or be assimilated out of recognition. We sometimes speak as though the real enemy of Christianity were ignorance or apathy. There is ignorance enough and apathy enough. But the real enemy is more positive and deadly than these. The real enemy is an aggressive and pagan creed which affirms that the chief end of man is to get the mastery over his fellows which comes from economic success. That faith is so potent, it has so great a prestige, that it is not too much to call it a religion. That religion lies at the very center of our industrial organization. Only a mighty and genuine faith can ever defeat it. If Christians are to overcome this antichrist of to-day, they must do more than mouth harmless generalities. They must strike at the very center of the pagan creed itself and refuse to be browbeaten by talk of economic expediency and refuse to distrust the social ethics of their own faith. This distrust and timidity have made the churches comparatively impotent in the most important areas of life.

There are in the main three things which the church may well keep in mind, in its effort to establish a more Christian order.

The first is negative, but of crucial importance; that is, not to allow itself to become infected with this gospel of prosperity. Julien Benda, the European philosopher, has written a striking book which he calls *The Treason of the Intellectuals*. In it he protests against those who have shared in spiritual and intellectual culture accepting the domination of nationalist politicians. He says, "The clerk," using that word in its medieval sense of an educated man, "who becomes a narrow, nationalistic patriot becomes a traitor." He calls such people "the spiritual militia of the temporal power." "The effect of the mobilization of the intellectuals of the world behind a series of separate national flags is to render impossible a world of learning, one world bent on a general search after truth." That is a striking phrase—"the spiritual militia of the temporal power." That is exactly what Christians become when their chief allegiance is to the reign of an economic philosophy rather than to Jesus. There is a story in *Sinbad the Sailor* of a ship which sailed so near to the magnetic mountain that all the nails which held its parts together were drawn out by the magnetism of the mountain and the ship sank. It is possible for a church to come into such close proximity to a magnetic mountain whose pull consists not in iron but in silver and gold, that the principles which hold it together as a church of Christ are drawn out. A church which forgets or does not take seriously the uncompromising ideal and teaching of Jesus must be content with a watered down adaptation of Jesus. It is sometimes even reduced to taking its religion from Bruce Barton and its ethics from Roger Babson.

A second line of advance is to support the growing challenge directed against this ascendency of business profits, which protests, not so much in the name of ethics or even humanity but in the name of sound economics. To many of the keenest thinkers of our time, the desire for immediate profits encumbers industry in the services which it might render, like an Old Man of the Sea. In eloquent and moving words Stuart Chase voices this protest:

A beautiful technique this new science of management; the crowning achievement of prosperity. Given a free hand it might remake American industry humanely as well as technically. Given a free hand it might abolish poverty, immeasurably diminish the stresses and strains which have dogged every step of the industrial revolution since the days of Watt. It might flood the nation with essential and even beautiful goods at a fraction of their present cost, raise the curse of Adam, and lay the basis for if not positively usher in one of the noblest civilizations which the world has ever seen.

But the hands of management are not free. The technician is constantly undone by the sales department, which, floundering in a pecuniary economy, sees no other way—and, indeed, there is no other way—to maintain capacity than by style changes, annual models, advertising, misrepresentation, and high-pressure merchandising. He is undone by the vested interests of the owners, who demand their pound of flesh in rent, interest, and dividends *now*, with no thought for the rounded perfection of engineering principles, and the time which they—and the physical laws which sanction them—demand.

Here is an ally of tremendous power and possibilities in the fight for a better order, a trend bearing out the statement of George Bernard Shaw that "the demands of Jesus are turning out to be good sense and sound economics."

3

In the third place it is imperative to remember that the only way to keep from being infected by the gospel of success is the positive one, of holding and proclaiming Jesus' own message clearly—the insistence on co-operation instead of competition, the service of one another in place of profit motivation, the sense of fellowship with man and God for prosperity as the end of life.

CHAPTER VII

THE GOSPEL OF SALESMANSHIP

THE present economic pattern in which we all move, what has been called the "gospel of mass-production," is perfectly familiar. It is an economy closely geared together combining the processes of manufacture, based on the multiplication of separate units, known as mass-production. It is supported by mass-consumption, the process involving the intermediate forces of the standardization of taste as well as products, and mass-stimulation through advertising and other forms of pressure.

The process goes—produce more, earn more, spend more, add to production, and thus to wages and consequent expenditure. It is a merry-go-round; a circle. Mass-production, with its prodigious output, involving applied skill and standardized products, depends in turn upon mass-stimulation of new wants and identical tastes, and on the elevation of salesmanship, with all the forces of psychology turned on the public, to exorcise the black demon of sales resistance, the villain in the drama, a shadowy but menacing ghost which stands at the side threatening to jam the machinery and stop the merry-go-round.

This process is being exported to other lands. Our question here is not so much what it is doing for trade—but the question, What is it doing for life?

The growing literature of protest and critical examination of the cost of supporting this great economic machine measured in terms of human life and comfort and character brings reminders of another historic discussion of a machine.   That was the heated controversy which resulted from the appearance of the Wooden Horse before the gates of Troy.   Immediately Troy was divided into two parties.   "Here is our salvation," cried one.   "Here is our undoing," cried the other.   In like manner— the machine and mass-consumption have created two parties to-day.   On the one hand, the apologists for the glories of mass-consumption become poets, in many cases.   Their praises grow lyrical in character.   A striking instance of this is to be found in Garet Garrett's book, *The American Omen*. It would be hard to find anywhere quite such lyrical ecstasy since Shelley's *Ode to the West Wind*.   He sees a new era which has already dawned on human life, through the multiplication of vacuum cleaners, electric ice boxes, and the thousand and one other contrivances which he lumps together under the name "human values."   Nothing else comes into the picture.

On the other hand we hear voices which sound like Cassandra, or, to find a contrast to Shelley, like Thomson's *City of Dreadful Night*.

With the high-wages theory of production, based on the belated realization that commodities must have purchasers, and that these purchasers must have both money and leisure with which to consume, there have come large benefits of an ethical sort as well as for production.   It has brought possibilities, often realized, of a higher standard of living, increase in comfort, dignity, and cultural and spiritual opportunities. In both social and economic wisdom it is a tremendous advance beyond the long venerated idol of the iron law of wages. As we shall see later, in the operation of this process human values are often crowded out under the necessity of keeping the wheels turning. Nevertheless, there are real ethical and spiritual values to be considered.

The chorus of enthusiastic cheer leaders over the present situation is to be criticized, not because of any grudging attitude toward the goal of high wages, but because their ecstasy is often very premature. We find a gross overestimate of the extent to which high wages have actually been applied. Also there is a frequent overestimate of the strength which this high-wage theory would have against a serious depression. Let some slip in the gear-box of the big machine occur, how solidly would the high wage hold? Would there not be, rather, rapid adoption of that version of the theory which now is so largely adopted—"A fine theory—for the other fellow! Let him pay the high wages so that his workers will have more money to buy my products, while I continue to produce at a low cost."

There has been as yet on a wide scale only a very casual look at the human consequences of a system dependent on what may be called "forced consumption." The tyranny of life which occurs when man is regarded almost wholly as a producer has been clearly realized, but the tyranny which comes when man is regarded primarily as a consumer has not been as clearly seen. It is, of course, hard to separate production from consumption in estimating its human results; they are tied together like two wheels joined by a connecting belt. Looking at both, three consequences clearly appear—its drive, its waste, and the pressure which the system makes for the confinement of life into the activities and interests of making and buying.

This latter leads to the smothering of those personal values which are beyond the mere means of sustaining life; in other words, in terms of the figure used earlier, those values represented by a picture rather than the frame in which it is set.

When we speak of the drive of production, much more is included than the familiar scene of the high-speed production belt set at a rate too high. That is a large item in the indictment. But the inhuman drive is not confined to the factory. It includes all the processes which compel a demand for the products of the factory; thus it becomes a major force affecting the whole life of a people. There is an invisible belt running out from the factory turning the wheels of millions of lives. The man who makes automobiles is not the only one who feels it. The man who sells the machine is driven relentlessly also. He is forced to get rid of so many cars a month by any means of pressure he can summon, or else lose the agency. At the other end of the process the consumer is driven. He is caught in the toils of all the stimulation which may be brought to induce him to Buy! buy! buy! Reinhold Niebuhr has pointed out that the storekeeper, struggling to keep above water under the obstacles of an extended credit system, is also driven.

A second indictment is the appalling waste of

national resources such as oil and lumber. Even greater in volume is the waste that is deliberately made by changing styles and the technique of obsolescence—forcing the scrapping of articles with long use still in them. Added to that is the enormous waste of distribution.

Consider some, at least, of the broad and obvious aspects of the consequences to the mind-attitude of a people of an economy resting to so large an extent on salesmanship. The vicious character of the circle of mass-production which can be kept going only by the high pressure of stimulation and consequent mass-consumption, is to be seen in the fact that it is hard to determine whether we produce for the sake of consumption or consume for the sake of production, though in large degree the emphasis at present seems to be on the latter. It is no exaggeration to say that we have come into a real new order; it is not so much a process of supplying actual needs as to find consumers for things produced. First comes the production often going it blind; then buyers must be found to keep the wheels going; and the result is that man is turned into a buyer. Human beings become mainly prospects; our greatest national industry becomes the production of new wants.

Greater and greater consumption has received excited praise from those who hail the multiplication of wants and purchases in the mood of the aged Simeon in the Temple—"Now lettest thou thy servant depart in peace, . . . for mine eyes have seen thy salvation." Witness the apocalyptic words of a book with a characteristic title, *Selling Mrs. Consumer*, by Christine Frederick.

Our new vision of increased consumption and consumer welfare has been the guiding touchstone of our work and is a matchless contribution which America can hope to make to greatness in civilization, the spread of wealth in the form of goods for consumption to all classes to a degree never known before and on a principle which is a complete overturning of all hard-and-fast principles. Consumption is the name given to the new doctrine; and it is admitted to-day to be the greatest idea America has to give to the world; the idea that workmen and the masses are not looked upon simply as workers, or producers, but as consumers; . . . pay them more, sell them more, prosper more is the equation.

Now, the core of that, of course, is nothing but the insight of J. A. Hobson and others, recorded long before it was generally recognized or adopted in America, that the cause of bad trade is underconsumption. Whether Hobson would have regarded the mass of agencies for forcing buying as a necessary corollary of his theory is very much to be doubted.

We have had an ironical extension of Thomas Carlyle's plea for production which would make Thomas turn over in his grave. "Produce! produce!" he called, "if it be but the most infinitesimal atom of a product, in God's name produce it!" Industrialism has nailed his words up in the office and factory as a slogan, and producers, whether in God's name or not, form myriads of infinitesimal atoms up to sixteen-cylinder automobiles. Consumers must be found. If they are so unpatriotic and heretical as to show symptoms of a buyer's strike, the heavy artillery of stimulation and advertising is brought up to "batter down sales resistance." Forced sales to consumers of what they do not want, and do not really need, in comparison with other more essential needs, are a basic part of the process. Under the pressure mechanical contrivances, new styles, luxuries of various degrees and kind take precedence, in multitudes of families, over human needs and comforts not only of a cultural sort but of an actual physical kind. Readers of *Middletown* cannot but have been impressed by scores of descriptions of workers' homes—ugly, dirty, inconvenient, in which expensive appliances have been purchased on installment payments at prices out of all proportion to what they contribute to comfort and happiness, while food, clothing, and housing are meager.

Mr. Matthew Josephson has conceived this forced consumption as a Dragon which must be fed.

If I may become allegorical for a moment, I would say that there is a monster, a Dragon in a cave, to whom the Arcadians must daily bring sacrifices in order to incur their heavily mortgaged bliss.

One caught glimpses of the Dragon everywhere; by the banks of the Monongahela in Pittsburgh I saw poisonous smoke shooting from his nostrils, red flame from the furnace of his jaws. You may see him in Gary, near Chicago; in Akron; in Newark; in Birmingham, Alabama; in Seattle. He has become monstrously big and strong; terribly armed, he must be given more and more to combat; and, terribly hungry, he must be given more and more to consume. To the Dragon of mass-industry must be brought the sacrifices of our personal freedom, of independence of thought and will; individual tendencies must give way to mass needs and activities.

Under this pressure to buy, buy, buy, we have rewritten our Shakespeare and the famous passage in

"As You Like It" on the "Seven Ages of Man" as an interpretation of life comes out something like this:

All the world's a market place,
And all the men and women merely buyers.
They have their purchases and deferred payments.
And one man in his time supports many salesmen.
His acts being seven ages.   At first the infant—
A prospect for the dairy industry and infant's wear.
And then the whining schoolboy, with his satchel,
        creating a demand for leather goods and
Textbooks, with frequent profitable changes.
And then the lover, needing a sport model coupé;
Helping the jewelry trade and those dispensing
Three-room suites of furniture, on easy payments.
And then the soldier, stabilizing a healthy activity
        among munition manufacturers and uniform
        makers.
And then the justice, likeliest prospect of all,
Target for an army of builders, furnishers and
        investment brokers.
And so he plays his part.   The sixth act shifts—
Into the lean and slippered pantaloon,
But still a field for the shoe and pantaloon industry.
Last scene of all is second childishness,
The ideal time to buy a radio, with a
        Florentine cabinet—a bargain at two hundred
        dollars.

When we speak of pressure we do not think entirely of its external form.   The outside stimulation is applied to deep-seated human motives, cleverly played upon by all the resources of psychology.   We have heard much of "invisible" government in the United States.   It is usually portrayed as a con-

spiracy of high finance. But the most effective
form of "invisible" government is not anything so
concrete, but something far more complete and effective.   It might be called the tyranny of the Joneses.
We threw off the tyranny of George III, but the
tyranny of Mr. and Mrs. Jones, our present rulers,
with whom we try to keep up, is very hard to escape.

The deep-seated passion for equality, far more
strong than that for liberty, has been made the
motive power for keeping up with the neighbors
and does much to keep our feet on the economic
treadmill, plying men, women, and children with all
the appeals urging to a higher material standard of
living.

This restless absorption in reaching a higher
material consumption plane has been called by
Mr. James Truslow Adams "the new frontier,"
which in our day is substituted for the goal of the
physical frontier and pursued with all the energy
and thrust power which the other goal called forth.

The devices which enforce this pressure are
familiar: the growth of advertising from an un-
developed, casual aid in making sales to one of the
largest industries in the country; the spread of
installment selling and the application of the principle of "obsolescence"—the greatest incitement to
waste ever applied in the world's history.

Obsolescence as a technique is new and can no
more be made the basis of a sound economics than
of a balanced human life. Durability is the last
quality which many manufacturers try to impart to a
product. Long use, which was the chief appeal of
many articles in a former day, is anathema. To
make goods undesirable while there is still use in

156 JESUS AND THE AMERICAN MIND

them is a cardinal principle of forced buying. Each
year brings new models in automobiles and radios
and a thousand other products. In the automobile
a large part of the newness is in shining gadgets of
one sort and another which involve no fundamental
improvement in the car but are enough to stimulate
discontent and envy and a desire for purchase.

All the periods of history are ransacked to stimulate the passion to get something new and up to date.
Radio sets jump from Florentine styles one year to
Elizabethan the next, with a mid-season flurry
in Louis Quatorze. Alligator skin supplants snake
skin in shoes, with doubtless the rest of the reptile
family soon to be pressed into service. The lizard
and the ostrich had better hunt for cover. Skirts
drop four inches, and those who lack the inches
must stay at home after six o'clock in the evening.
All the colors of the rainbow and many which the
rainbow does not know are pressed into service.
"Hospital white" goes out of favor for bathroom
fixtures, and tiling of orchid, faun, coral, jade, and
cerise are accepted as "*the* thing," causing a fresh
turnover, literally and figuratively, in the plumbing
business. Even the humble utensils of the kitchen
get out of date by having the wrong color scheme—
a great advance over the naïve, simple days when
a coffee mill passed from one generation to
another!

To give an extra push to the glorious urge, Henry
Ford roundly berates thrift, to the applause of all
the salesmen in the country.

Bruce Barton, as usual, gives a deeply religious
interpretation. In a syndicated editorial at Christmas time he sings this carol to bigger and bigger sales:

So business begins to grow better at Christmas time, for every Christmas purchase helps to start the machinery of selling and making into quicker motion. "It is more blessed to give than to receive," said the Founder of Christmas, and he quoted sound political economy as well as great religious truth.

"Educate the world and his wife to want," cries one enthusiastic optimist, as he tosses his hat into air, "and the productive competency of the country will actually groan under the burden of the economic demand." ("Groan" is good!) "There is no theoretical limit to the general consumption possibilities." Closely associated with this technique and in indispensable support of it, is installment selling. We are not considering it from the economic side, but as a force influencing the life and mentality of a people. The American householder is the modern Atlas holding up the world, or as much as may be represented by an automobile, piano, vacuum cleaner, radio, furniture, jewelry. Installment selling had a modest beginning in the United States in a panic in 1873, as a temporary device to tide over the piano and organ industry. The tide has risen. It is estimated that the population of the nation is $600,000,000 in debt for installment purchases. Will Rogers has made a very ingenious solution of all traffic problems—simply keep all unpaid-for cars off the road! The extent to which we are dependent on consumption to the limit and beyond is illustrated in the appeal made by President Hoover in the stock crash in the fall of 1929 to everyone to "buy as much as possible."

Into this picture come two of the most powerful and persistent forces playing on the American mind—

salesmanship and advertising.   Joseph Jastrow calls
the elevation of salesmanship to its present pin-
nacle of homage the "American idol of the market
place."   The degree to which we are thinking and
talking in terms of salesmanship may be gauged by
the play of the word "sell" in our everyday vocabu-
lary.   It resounds with the tiresome thump of a
flat wheel on a trolley car.   We are told we must
sell "ourselves"; we must sell "ideas"; parrotlike
churchmen talk of "selling religion"; education
must likewise be "sold."   "I am not sold on it" is
the approved declaration of suspended judgment.
It is a shrewd comment of Edgar Mowrer that where
the consumption of goods has the prestige of a religion, the offering of them has a sacerdotal function.
From that springs the conception of salesmanship
as "service" with a sort of mystical halo about it.

The point at issue here is, of course, not the
natural and indispensable activity of selling, but its
exaltation and its pressure which have undeniably
laid waste our powers.   In Professor Jastrow's
words, "Let us render appreciatively unto salesmanship what is salesmanship's and render unto the goods
of choicer values the homage that is due goods that
make life worth provisioning."   It has often been
said that we have quite enough courses given on
"How to *Break Down* Sales Resistance."   What we
need more is a technique of "How to *Build Up* Sales
Resistance."   That is coming to be more and more a
large and fundamental task in Christian education.

The advertising man has become to an extensive
degree the guide, philosopher, and friend of the
millions.   That pre-eminence is a real threat to the
supremacy or even the continuance in any effective

degree of some essential Christian attitudes. Force utilizing every available science is applied to stimulating the desire for things, until, whatever the formal adherence to the supremacy of spiritual values one may have, the practical effect is to establish the assumption that life *does* consist in abundance of things. More than a billion dollars is spent in advertising in the United States every year. Directly and indirectly, six hundred thousand men and women are in the business of stimulating the desire for more and more things. "People are wasted by the hundred thousand upon the work of selling to other people things they neither want nor need because excess power has made excess things and means to make excess profits." The astounding success of propaganda during the Great War and particularly of the advertising of Liberty Loans, combined with mass-production so largely developed since the war, brought an undreamed of power and importance to advertising. To that, of course, must be added the way in which the excess profits' tax during the war increased the money available for advertising.

It is this excessive power, with the relentless assault on eye and ear, its frequent absurd and mendacious fairy tales, rather than the normal and legitimate function of the salesmanship in print, which is the impact making for a materialistic interpretation of life.

It is hard to estimate the effects of the steady pounding of "Buy this," "Buy that." The conflict between this unremitting force and the basic attitudes emphasized by Jesus was expressed recently by a man who told of spending a summer Sunday

morning in a little New Hampshire church. The
preacher was giving an exposition based on the
early part of the Sermon on the Mount, the passage
beginning "Consider the lilies." The effect upon
him was to sharpen as never before the feeling
that Jesus was everlastingly right in his insistence
on freedom from preoccupation with the lust for
material things. In the afternoon the man went
down to Boston on a railroad train and in a seat
picked up a copy of the Saturday Evening Post.
As he turned over the hundred and more pages
generously filled with advertisements which almost
screamed of the necessity of this thing and that
thing to life, he felt a force at work which made
simple living an enormously difficult achievement.
Add to that the advertisements of the billboards,
our "national folk lore," as someone has called them,
and that pillar of fire by night to lead us into the
promised land in the possession of things—the
illuminated electric advertising sign. All conspire
to develop the feeling that life is an empty and
aching blank if we do not have the thing they
advertise. Much emphasis has been laid, and
rightly, on the increase of honesty in advertising.
In many respects there is a far advance on the old
days of transparent trick and fraud. Much credit
for that must be given to the Federal Food and Drug
Act, but much belongs also to the efforts of self-
respecting advertisers. But with a great deal of
national advertising to-day there is a conscienceless
working on the suggestability of "innocents abroad."
It is seen in its worst form in cigarette advertising—
impertinent, untruthful, grotesque. Even Edward
L. Bernays, one of the stoutest proponents of the

propaganda and advertising, says that the business man recognizes that "he must not disregard entirely the methods of Barnum in reaching the public."

A very definite anti-Christian force in advertising is in the steady appeal to unethical motives, to promote the sale of luxuries. All sorts of motives in deadly antagonism to the Christian ethical ideal are resorted to. Envy, pride, ostentation, the love of splurge, the desire for precedence are appealed to in a subtle form, thus building up by insidious means a type of character far removed from that which Jesus sought to create. "Do you want your neighbors to envy you?" reads one automobile advertisement. The answer implied is, "Of course, any man in his right mind wants his neighbors to envy him." The means of securing that beautiful end is simply buy a Blank Blank Straight Eight and drive up the street and stop in front of your house and the neighbors will all go up in a wisp of green smoke!

Here is an advertisement inserted in the New York Times by the Atlanta, Georgia, Chamber of Commerce, appealing to business men to locate plants in Atlanta. In the three sentences quoted there are two thoroughly unethical motives appealed to. One, the possibility of exploiting labor, and the other a delicately aimed appeal to race and nationalistic prejudices.

For one thing I didn't believe labor could work the way these boys do down here. We certainly couldn't get the production per man in the old town—and I know you don't get it at your plant. Say what you please about the melting pots, the good old Anglo-Saxon race knows how to give work for wages.

Some of the most thoroughly vicious examples of this type of advertising have been put out by correspondence schools. With unreserved and unashamed blatancy they have preached the gospel of financial success as the supreme prize of life. One widely published advertisement a few years ago told the story of two boys who started out in life together. One was a success. He sat behind a mahogany desk and pushed a buzzer. The other was a failure. The words blazoned forth the ignominy of the failure at the top of the advertisement—"He lived in a side street!" And he was pictured living a simple, inconspicuous life with his family, the inference being that such a failure was a loathsome object. The magazines are full of such advertisements. It would be hard to find a more diabolically effective preaching of a pagan gospel.

A great deal of this may seem to some readers like a hopeless, quixotic attack on an inevitable order of life. In that very word "inevitable" is the crux of difficulty. It is accepted as inevitable— this regimentation, the insistence on prosperity, even without peace, content, or happiness or moral dignity. Many accept this because it means taking the line of least resistance for themselves. They regard as a finality what may be a temporary order. The criticism here expressed is not a diatribe against trade, not a romantic assumption that men can exist almost as disembodied spirits. It is, rather, a recognition that in the present massive stimulation of consumption there is a force at work molding multitudes into attitudes and desires which are in thoroughgoing antagonism to a primary emphasis of Jesus. If we go through the Sermon on the Mount, and those first talks of Jesus with his disciples, we cannot escape the conclusion that two primary attitudes which Jesus sought to establish in man were trust in God and freedom from a destroying preoccupation with things. "All these things do the Gentiles seek," Jesus said. Or, as Moffatt translates it, "Pagans make all that their aim in life." This to Jesus was essential paganism. Against that he set forth the mastery of one all-powerful rival preoccupation—"*Seek ye first the kingdom of God.*"

For people frequently achieve at one and the same time a higher standard of living and a lower standard of life. The cult of comfort crowds out the disposition to sacrifice for unselfish ends of life, a disposition which is the very core of Christianity. The line of criticism here expressed is simply a protest against burying the New Testament under the advertising pages of a Sunday newspaper.

The important thing is to see the antagonism— and more clearly than most people in the churches at present see it; to see that preoccupation with goods, not as something for the church to accept and bless, mitigating its blight here and there, a little, but as something to be confronted, challenged, and controlled; and not to allow the eminent respectability and wide acceptance of the force to disguise from our eyes its essentially antagonistic nature.

Again, insofar as the individual and family can do anything, it is clear that an understanding of the results in character and life of this pressure toward maximum consumption should make evident a duty of standing against the stream. There must be a personal declaration of independence; a high resolution that life shall not be lost in the process of

providing a physical basis for it. Especially, that
the house must not be allowed to swallow up the
home—an almost inevitable result of the slavery to a
higher standard of living.

Looking more widely on the social scene, it is for
those who see the threat to the Christian conception
of life to make common cause with the thinkers who
are criticizing this gospel of pressure-consumption,
both from the standpoint of economics and from a
concern for the humane and cultural values of life,
such critics, for instance, as Stuart Chase, James
Truslow Adams, R. H. Tawney, and Harry F. Ward.

Prosperity is confused with mere activity. An
artificially created "out-of-dateness," as the support
of prosperity, is a weak reed. A nation's wealth can
never be firmly or permanently founded on a combination of wastefulness and borrowing. Stuart
Chase has voiced this protest with brutally clear
words: "It still escapes me why a prosperity founded
on forcing people to consume what they do not need
and often do not want is, or can be, a healthy or
permanent growth. There will be an enormous
explosion when and if it cracks, but in the end we
may secure something nearer to the heart's desire."

In addition to this nothing less will suffice than to
make all the additional force possible to the demand
coming from many angles for a more rational social
direction of industry, a co-ordination of production
which will not leave basic needs unmet, while energy
is drained off into the production of unessentials, and
elaborate jimcracks, and contrivances which in turn
must be disposed of by forces which do violence to
higher values of life.

CHAPTER VIII

THE MENTAL LOCK STEP

A LINK in the circle of mass-production and consumption is, of course, standardization. Our interest here is not in the application of standardization to industrial processes, except for the necessary recognition that it is standardization of tastes which has made possible mass-production and the frequent consequence in speeding up with its evils in the exploitation of workers. It is not the standardized tools, and even products, but standardized thinking which most directly affects our present inquiries. Let it be said at once that probably no subject has been handled in recent years with more tiresome reiteration, exaggeration, and unchecked sarcasm. C. E. M. Joad, the British philosopher, for instance, writes joyously from the other side of the water of the "Babbit warren," and draws a heart-breaking picture of life in the United States—a drab procession of convicts in which every step is measured, every mouthful prescribed, and every thought dressed in a uniform. Alas, alas!

Even as a physical matter standardization is a process hard to measure accurately or estimate fairly in its social effects. The picture of America as the home of monotony has been vastly overdrawn; that it has left out of view strong tendencies making for variety and change is without question. It is quite easy, however, to swing to the other extreme, and in placid complacency overlook the extensive development of the habit of conformity in the United States, a habit and attitude widespread and deep-set, which make one of the most formidable obstacles to the sharp peculiarity of Christian teaching when it cuts across some of the main currents of our time. The inertia developed and strengthened by general mind-set toward an easy conformity to majority opinion, is one of the chief ethical liabilities of the present age.

To whatever extent mass-thinking prevails, it is partly due to the uniformity of articles for use and a standardization of tastes and habits of living on which mass-production rests for its success. More important, however, has been the enormous development of the machinery for creating uniform opinion which the last twenty-five years has brought. In a real sense the nation has reached a new birth-day in the development of these agencies for regimenting the population into a mental lock step. The movies, the radio, the syndicated newspapers, the demonstration which war propaganda made of the possibility of molding the minds of millions after one pattern—a lesson thoroughly learned and never forgotten — have had a very far-reaching influence. Someone asked Jane Addams not long ago what she thought of bobbed hair for girls. She replied that she was not worried about the uniformity on the outside of the heads of people; it was the uniformity on the inside which bothered her. It is something which should bother everyone with a concern for social progress, for there are large groups of the population which have minds just about as much alike as Ford parts.

The German philosopher, R. M. Freienfels, in his strangely named book *The Mysteries of the Soul*, expresses the harm and danger of mass-thinking when he says that "it substitutes the cheap democracy of equality for the noble democracy of liberty." That is a penetrating observation on one of the strongest influences in American life. There is a cheap democracy of equality, eager for and satisfied with likeness to the majority, content to be turned out mentally and physically in the season's model. Inevitably the noble democracy, more intent on liberty, is subordinated. There is a Gresham's law in democracy as well as in finance; cheap money displaces the more valuable, and cheap democracy tends to drive out the better—as a glance at the infringement of civil liberties in the United States in the last fifteen years will readily show.

These forces for making people think as well as eat, wear, and use the same thing, have induced a reverence for majority opinion. Douglas Woodruff says that most Americans do not mind dying, for that means joining the great majority. This characteristic attitude is like a barricade against new social experiments and new forms of thought which oppose accepted dogmas. "Twenty million people can't be wrong"—this popular slogan, so dear to the advertiser, expresses that blighting reverence. That this impressive banality just quoted flies in the face of history can be readily answered by Henry Ford's trenchant aphorism, "History is bunk." James Bryce pointed out years ago that free thought is our weak point, and since that time the means of enforcing conformity to set patterns of thinking have been enormously magnified.

Turn to *Middletown*, for a picture of the mediocre level of the mental and spiritual life which is characteristic of a large cross section of America.   Here is a progressive community, prosperous in the accepted sense of volume of trade, of corporation profits, bank clearings, but here is a documented picture of a "community easily led by the nose, living on slogans and clichés, political, moral and religious, easily victimized by propaganda and satisfied with quack remedies."   The redeeming criticism which might have been expected in theory from schools, from churches, from other agencies, is entirely snuffed out.

In two respects this tendency to regiment thinking into a mental lock step presents a formidable antagonism to the task of making a more Christian social order.

The first is the rigorous pressure to enforce orthodox opinion, economic and social.   William Temple, Archbishop of York, making a general observation on democracy, has described a development which has taken place to a pronounced degree in the United States, "Democracy by its machinery tends to produce herd-mentality with pugnacity of spirit, and what we have to try to do with our educational work is the exact opposite, which is independence of mind and fellowship of the spirit.   It is extremely difficult to do and more worth doing than anything else."   "Herd-mentality with pugnacity of spirit" (the picture suggests a stampede of angered buffaloes) —those words are an exact description of a hundred drives since the Great War, from the lawless violation of the constitutional rights in Attorney General Palmer's red raids in 1919-20 and the large traffic in slander and defamation carried on by professional patriots, to the subtle social and economic pressure by which multitudes are kept to the task of trying to look, talk, and act like the president of the local Chamber of Commerce.

"For nonconformity," said Emerson, "the world whips you with its displeasure." The business of whipping for nonconformity has had a development Emerson never dreamed of. The lash has a very long reach; it keeps a much larger crowd in line. Miss Maude Royden on her return to England after her last visit to America said that it was not true that there were more fools in the United States than in other countries; the difference was that in the United States "the fools were organized." That is a hard saying, but it is headed in the direction of truth. A pugnacity of spirit organized to enforce adherence to the least common denominator in social and political thinking is an effective bulwark against advance. The shameful story of the violation of civil liberties in the United States since the Great War and the lethargy and lack of indignation with which such violations have usually been regarded by a majority of the population, make it evident that the "noble democracy of liberty" has ceased to be a first love. Not the least part of the shame of the story lies in the fact that the churches have felt and expressed on the whole so little concern for the preservation of civil liberties and respect for the rights of minority groups. In their zeal for the Eighteenth Amendment to the Constitution many churchmen give the impression that so far as they are concerned it is the only amendment. Had they but served the first ten amendments involving the Bill of Rights with half the zeal they served the eighteenth, American history in the last ten years would have had fewer black spots. For that lack of interest and effort means that there has been an inadequate recognition of how closely civil liberties are tied in to the whole Christian conception of the divine worth of man.

A second aspect of standardized thinking which has a close relation to the Christian task is the fact that the building of the kingdom of God will never be accomplished by timid or conventional minds. As it was in the beginning it is now and ever shall be—"We must obey God rather than man." The apostolic task is the same to-day as on the day of Pentecost—that of turning the world upside down. The church will not get very far with that enterprise if it must depend on people who think it is right side up at present, men and women to whom respectability and conformity to prevailing winds of doctrine are first requisites of life, and that is exactly the type of character which is being developed in large numbers. In earliest days of childhood the forming of herd-mindedness is begun. It is continued through adolescence. In the action of most of the agencies of religious education no effective counteractive to this prevailing type of mind is developed. The result is that when the ideas of Jesus cut across accepted social and economic dogmas, there is little disposition to follow him. The Son of man becomes the sort of Son familiar to political conventions, where a "favorite son is one you have made up your mind to abandon after the third ballot." No task of education or training rests more heavily on the churches than that of building up against the blighting habit of conformity that essential Christian trait of intelligent and daring nonconformity, not for the sake of eccentricity, but in loyalty to the Great Nonconformist.

What instrument of social and psychological measurement could be devised so delicate that it could record accurately the power of nationalism in shaping the present mind and spirit of the American people? It is easy enough to pick out facts which will pass as support for extreme views of the matter. At one extreme there is the frequently expressed interpretation that an assertive nationalism is rapidly supplanting Christianity as our religion; that the state is receiving the unquestioning veneration usually associated with religion. At the other end of the argument are marshaled the undeniable evidences of wider international outlook which are pressed into the service of the view that narrow-minded patriotism is giving way to world-mindedness.

The opposition of these extremes is to be explained by two trends which are running side by side. One is the reactionary trend—always a legacy of war—toward a new national self-consciousness and aggressive assertion. The other is the equally well defined movement toward an international consciousness and the organization of world peace. As usual, much depends on our definition. Inevitable confusion has come from the use of the word "nationalism" with different senses. It has been used as an equivalent of "patriotism," the love of the country which has created forces of immeasurable ethical and spiritual worth. "Nationalism," when used to represent an antagonistic force to the internationalism concerned with the welfare of the world as well as of one's own nation, has perhaps never been more adequately described than by Professor Carlton J. H. Hayes:

Nationalism is a proud and boastful habit of mind about one's nation, accompanied by a supercilious or hostile attitude toward other nations; it admits that individual citizens of one's country may do wrong, but it insists that one's nationality or national state is always right. Nationalism is either ignorant, or prejudiced, or inhuman, or jaundiced; in both cases it is a form of mania, a kind of extended and exaggerated egotism, and it has easily recognizable symptoms of selfishness, intolerance, and jingoism, indicative of delusions of grandeur from which it suffers. Nationalism is artificial and it is far from ennobling; in a word, it is patriotic snobbery.

It is this virile and aggressive force which deserves the description which Doctor Fosdick gives it, "Christianity's greatest rival." That it is a real and powerful force molding the mind cannot be denied by anyone who lives in the United States whose eyes and ears are open. J. A. Spender says that he considers the Chicago Tribune tower as a symbol of America, glittering and dazzling. Perhaps. But it is the legitimate symbol of forces playing upon the American people, forces by no means glittering and dazzling, unless we have in mind the tawdry and specious glitter of the perverted patriotism of the motto which flies at the mast head of the Tribune editorial columns—"My country, may she ever be right, but right or wrong, my country." It is a symbol of a jingoistic spirit, cynical of ideals, not scorning to defame those who seek to embody ideals, which steadily endeavors to build up narrow and bigoted attitudes to other nations and to efforts for international co-operation. This abnormal conception of the state has had a very real elevation to the place of an effective religion. Perhaps the description given of this promotion of nationalism into the ranks of religion given by Professor J. A. Lasswell, of the University of Chicago, may seem like an exaggerated caricature, but it has lines easily identified in many organizations, and movements, and so-called patriotic "drives." Professor Lasswell says:

The vogue of superheated nationalism is attributed to the fact that the upper middle classes have discovered in it an emotional substitute for Christianity. What is happening in America and elsewhere is a process of syncretism by which an ever-diminishing element of Christianity and an ever-increasing element of nationalism are entering into the alloy known as modern religion.

The god of the new cult is the patria, the state, for whom the modern man will offer up his life. The ideal of the national state is a mighty, mystic power outside of puny individual men. It is the source of blessing for those who worship and obey. To propitiate and to serve is the highest duty of man. The national state has a mission, and its mission is everlasting.

The new religion has its rituals. The flag is supplanting the cross. The flag is the object of ceremonious salutes and dippings. Men bare their heads, children swear allegiance, adolescents orate, and the grand old chiefs of the tribe lend an ear to the wisdom of babes and sucklings. The national Christmas in America comes on the Fourth of July, the special days set aside for Saint George, Saint Abraham, Saint Theodore, Saint Woodrow. The manger lies at Mount Vernon; good can hail from Virginia. The devout adorn their walls with icons, and upon their terraces lie busts.

The growth of nationalism is partly due, of course, to the natural aftermath of the Great War. Hatred and fear, deliberately stirred up, must have an outlet. When the war ended, there were in the United States not only vast reservoirs of unused guns and bullets; there were vast reservoirs of unexpended hate and pugnacity. There was a frantic search for a new enemy against which to organize "alarums and excursions." Indeed, for many patriots the years following the war abounded in more thrills than the war itself, for a rather strikingly large proportion of the most ardent of those professional patriots were unavoidably detained at home during the actual hostilities. The American Defense Society tried to keep the war going with a campaign against German goods, solemnly warning against poisonous germs and other diabolical evils. But this campaign never got very far. Russia promised much more excitement. Germany in a political sense was too evidently dead, but Russia was thrillingly alive and full of Bolshevists. So, aided by the Department of Justice, the big gun of the card catalogue was drawn up and placed in position, and a barrage of charges of Bolshevism was laid down, spattering its paper bullets all over the country. The Ku Klux Klan waxed strong in such an atmosphere, where the residue of hate fell on Negroes, foreigners, Catholics, and Jews.

That fever has passed its crisis, much to the regret of many professionals thrown out of an exhilarating occupation. Its most pernicious aftermath is the enormous increase given to militarism through the extension of military training in schools and colleges.

The opposite trend is the growth of an international feeling and consciousness, the breaking down of barriers of provincialism, the growing popular demand for co-operative efforts for peace and the limitation of armaments, the growing recognition by the churches of war as the supreme ethical and spiritual issue of the day—all these are genuine gains of the last twelve years. If we have had a growing imperialism in relation to the weaker nations of Central America, there has also been a formidable and realistic exposure of that imperialism, making a vivid contrast to the days, not so long ago, when it would have been rationalized as a pious and patriotic enterprise. If there has been an immense increase of military and naval strength and of military training, there has been a stubborn public opinion opposing the growth. One demonstration of the reality and power of this public opinion was the opposition which developed against the government's fatuous plan for a Defense Day, an opposition before which the plan was soon withdrawn in embarrassed confusion. The other occasion which demonstrated the strength of anti-war opinion was when inept diplomacy threatened to embroil us with Mexico. During the last year there has been an impressive volume of opinion against the proposed high tariff, based not so much on economic grounds as on the sure effect of such a tariff in developing international ill will.

Here is a genuine ferment of ideal forces not to be made by any means an excuse for a satisfying complacency, but evidence of the working of a potent yeast, a yeast which is veritable leaven of the kingdom of God.

No outlook upon the major forces in American life

which are in competition with and antagonism to the mind of Jesus could possibly leave out of consideration what is one of the most considerable, continuous, and insidious of all the influences playing upon the mentality and character of the population—the motion picture. Yet to estimate, even roughly, the mental and social effect of motion pictures would call for a piece of social research so large and ramifying that it has never been attempted. Quantitative studies of detailed areas of that influence have been made, notably on the effect of the motion pictures on groups of school children, but no research is adequate to measure the impact on the whole population —on ideas, tastes, standards, manners, and morals. But to say that it is as pervasive as the salt of the sea is to utter an accepted platitude.

The movies are typical of the complications which the machine age has brought to the moral and spiritual task of Christianity in that three of the characteristic forces of the age converge in the motion picture—the machine itself applied to art, the enormous stimulation of the profit motive, and standardization, both as cause and as effect. Here are the forces which have gone into the making of an agency of mental and moral influence unique in the world's history.

The extent of that influence is rather hard to exaggerate. The weekly attendance at motion picture theaters is variously estimated at from thirty to forty million. Mr. Will Hays makes the claim that the advent of the talking picture has increased the weekly attendance by 15,000,000. Stuart Chase estimates that there is spent on moving and talking pictures a billion and a half dollars a year. The *Film Year Book* says the invested capital of the motion

picture industry was a billion and a half dollars in
1927. There are to-day more than twenty-two
thousand motion picture theaters in the United
States.

It lies far beyond the province of this book to
attempt any estimate of the sociological effects of the
motion picture, or any evaluation of those effects as
socially good or bad. Such an attempt as the latter
would inevitably end in an oversimplification of a
complex force. All that can here be attempted is a
fragmentary indication of some of the most obvious
ethical liabilities which the motion pictures have
for the creation of the individual character and
personality, and social order bearing distinctively
Christian qualities. One of the first things to be
mentioned may seem rather remote, but it is basic
to the whole question of the mental capacities and
qualities of a people. That is the effect of the
"movies" in inducing lazymindedness. Earl Barnes
has put this liability very simply and clearly—tracing
its effect from earliest days on:

For educating youth nothing can take the place of all-
round sensuous contact with reality. When a boy goes
to the playground, the work shop, or out with the Boy
Scouts, he gains material to think with, and he does some
thinking. When the same boy goes to the ordinary
movies he may try to think, but he lacks the sensuous
experience to think with; his ideas cannot pass into action; he becomes habituated to fragments; he becomes
lazy-minded and substitutes feeling for thinking. He is
on the way to becoming a movie-fan, lazy-minded, fragmentary, emotional—a thrill hunter.

"Lazy-minded"—that makes poor soil for the
development of the capacity to think, to weigh, to

criticize, on which ultimately rests the whole enterprise of making a better order in individual and social
life.   That liability, with its vast ramifications in
social life, goes directly back to the making of
profit.   Motion pictures are costly.   Because of the
cost they must make great profits, and to make great
profits they must make a wholesale appeal.   That
means to the greatest common denominator in mentality.   Hence the easiest solution, the short-cut
to profit is to base the appeal on emotions which are
more universal and primitive than thinking.   The
business man, the moron, the child, are thus placed
on a common level, and the emotions dealing with
sex, avarice, hate, conflict, the stock emotions of
mother, home, and flag-waving are made the endlessly worked over stock-in-trade of the scenario
writer.   Expose forty million people a week to this
playing upon the emotions with a minimum of
thought required, with even that minimum done for
a person—and the result is bound to be a deadening
of mental alertness, a distaste for the painful
exertion of thinking and a growing incapacity
for it.

Unblushingly this whole stupefaction of mental
capacity and appetite is paraded in the advertising
of films. Here are a few picked out at random from
a Chicago newspaper—"A torrent of thrills"; "tum
tum music that beats with your heart beat, entices a
fast pulse that keeps your feet tapping"; "breath-
taking suspense which makes the chills run up and
down your backbone."

The point of attack is the heart beat and the backbone—the primitive. The frequent result is that
anything demanding the least concentration is dis-

missed as "high-brow," any rigor of mental exertion is severe and forbidding.

A second area of influence is in the effect on the mind of millions of the sheer inanity of an enormous volume of the film offerings. This is something entirely apart from the obscenity and vicious suggestiveness which form so large a count against the movies at the present time; but it is a question whether the ultimate effects are not as bad or worse. In his "Heraclitus, or the Future of the Films" Ernest Betts goes to the heart of the matter, the lack of honest art in the portrayal of life:

If films are to have any future as an art, there must be something serious behind them, some wisdom and pity, some passion and grandeur, above the mere story-telling capacity. At present the maker of films is not allowed to have any artistic integrity.

And where "artistic integrity" is lacking there is bound to be the substitution of unreal, crude distortions of life, of standards of taste which make for essential vulgarization. As another student of the film industry has expressed it, Terry Ramsaye:

The world of the motion picture includes few men of power who have any interest in either science, art, or culture for their own sake, and none who sees the screen in the light of such an interest. Their test of attainment is the auditor and the ticker. The movies have made money, and in the Broadway judgment that makes them perfect now.

The steady pressure of this force making for the distortion of significant values of life is portrayed in vivid but restrained words by S. K. Ratcliffe:

Think of American civilization as it is portrayed upon the screen, not in uncertain driblets but in a continued and overwhelming spate! It is surely appalling to reflect that literally nothing in the world to-day is so universally familiar to the vast multitude of our fellow creatures as the picture made of America by a small crowd of Americans and by them built up into one of the great international industries of the age. There it is: the crude imbecilities of the Wild West drama; the rawness of industrial production and business adventure, of cocktail parties, night clubs, the duel of sex, and the degradation of marriage.

Beyond this is the more obvious effect on the mind of millions in the incessant sexual suggestiveness which in the last three years has been growing steadily worse. It is so obvious that there is no need whatever to particularize in regard to it. Professor Edward A. Ross of the University of Wisconsin gives the expert estimate of a part of this influence in his judgment:

We have a generation of youth sex-exerted and self-assertive; and there can be no doubt that the arrival of overmastering sex desire in the boy's life has been antedated by at least two or three years, thanks to the abnormal and harmful stimulation of films.

The most hopeful aspect of the present situation in this regard is that multitudes of people have come to see through the pious propaganda of the Motion Picture Producers and Distributors organization. The movies are to be judged and are being judged not by the high-sounding ideals announced, but by actual performance.

Beyond this malignant and monstrous force in the most direct and fundamental way antagonistic to the Christian ideal of marriage and sexual morality is another influence, less obvious but just as sub-

versive of essential Christian evaluation of life.
This is part of the whole attitude discussed above
as The Religion of Prosperity. One of the surest
and most constant influences making for the spread
of this interpretation of life in terms of material
prosperity is the effective preaching of that gospel
to millions every week from the films. In The
New York World on April 2, 1930, there appeared an
editorial which so clearly analyzed the vicious moral
influence of this screen gospel that it is here quoted
in part. It is all the more effective for its purpose
in that it is not the plea of a preacher, but made
simply on the broad ground of a thoroughgoing
social morality:

The deepest evil of the movies does not arise from the
crooks, and the bedroom scenes, and the bathing girls,
but from a vicious falsification of human values. One
could censor out of the movies everything that Senator
Smoot and Mr. John Sumner might object to without
touching the immorality of the films. Such a censorship
would not touch the fact that the movies reflect a view
of life in which men have gotten rich so quickly and
furiously that they have lost all sense of the burden of
man's destiny. For what good is it to protect an adolescent boy or girl against seeing a too passionate embrace
on the screen if all the rest of the picture is devoted to
impressing them with the notion that they will be happy
if they have a Hollywood bungalow and a high-powered
motor? If the professional moralists had a little more
moral insight they would realize that this, the materialism of the movies, their constant celebration of the
acquisitive and competitive instincts, is far more deeply
degrading, even to the sexual life of an adolescent, than
ribaldry or coarseness.

Here and there a camera man, a director, a writer, an

actor, accidentally and incidentally does an honest and beautiful thing. But normally the monstrous wholesale profit-making machine grinds on and on, devouring the talents which it hires, and doing more to undermine taste and custom and popular integrity than schools, universities, and churches can hope to restore.

Here, then, is one of the major battlefields of the century from the point of view of the ethical and spiritual transformation of life. The first step is to recognize where the power of inertia and opposition to the Christian ideal lies, for on that step everything else depends. When that recognition of the deadly antagonism to the mind of Jesus, which now finds such vigorous expression in the movies, becomes clear and widespread, there will be more moral energy available to crystallize public opinion with an effective force. Some lines of action which that aroused moral energy might take when it arrives have been suggested by Mr. Fred Eastman. They include the refusal to trust any longer in the promises of the producers and of their organization to reform voluntarily and clean house; breaking the present monopoly which a few men now hold on the film business (one step in this is the passage of the Brookhart Bill now before the Senate which seeks to prevent "block booking" of films); the establishment of a federal motion picture commission; reform in motion picture advertising and selection by parents of films they allow their children to see, boycotting the unfit ones.

Perhaps the picture drawn in this chapter has seemed like a portrait of an insuperable antichrist. Frankly, it has been a one-sided picture, more space and attention being given to describing enemies than allies of the Christian purpose. But the picture has not been drawn in a pessimistic mood. It is no part of its conclusion that the enemies of the mind of Jesus are as giants and that those who seek to incarnate his mind in our life are as grasshoppers.

The beginning of successful efforts for a more ethical life is that we see the extent of the battle and do not underestimate the power of opposing forces. There is no hope unless we see that we are not in a sham battle. It is a stupendous but exhilarating task and the actual undertaking of it seriously will bring, as it always has brought, throughout Christian history, tremendous increase in resources. There is throughout the churches more or less observance of this year as the nineteen hundredth anniversary of Pentecost. One startling fact about Pentecost should never be forgotten. It was when the apostles faced the Pentecostal task that they received the Pentecostal power. There is a divine economy in the supplying of power. It is not given to those who do not need it, but to those who are facing a task which requires it. If we face the Pentecostal task in our own time, the very devotion and daring of that act will open new sources of power.

Nothing less can bring the mind of Jesus to our time than that his disciples, individually and gathered together in the church, shall make themselves at real cost the channel through which his message comes. That truth was set forth in a moving parable on the morning in January, 1930, when King George's speech opening the London Naval Conference was broadcast in the United States. Just a few moments before the speech was to come on, an official in the plant of the Columbia Broad-

casting Company, Mr. Walter Vivian, discovered
that something was the matter with the wiring.   He
realized that it would take twenty minutes to make
the repairs and that meanwhile thousands who were
listening for the King's speech would not hear him.
Without hesitation he grasped the ends of the broken
wires, one in each hand, to restore the circuit.   The
shock of the two hundred fifty volt charge and the
leakage of the current shook his arms and burned
his hands, but he held on while there went through
him the King's message of peace.

It is a costly task—this carrying of a royal message.   What was done with that message of the
English king is a symbol of the only way in which
God's message will be carried to the world.   That
is what Jesus did, "This is my body, which is broken
for you."   The disciple is not above his master.
Only through human lives will there ever be found
an effective medium for the carrying of a King's message of peace.

CHAPTER IX

JESUS AND A HOSTILE WORLD

IN the opening chapter of this book there was a reference to a mosaic taken from the catacombs of Rome of the third century, now on exhibition in the art gallery in Detroit. That bit of early Christian art, now shown in so strange an environment, was mentioned as the symbol of an essential antagonism between the faith it represented and some of the ruling motives of American industrialism. But it is more than the symbol of an existing conflict. It holds stirring suggestions and challenge for the whole enterprise of bringing the mind of Jesus into the mind of our time and environment.

Those who have followed the working out of the theme of this volume thus far may well be in the mood of Mr. Chesterton as he surveys the literature of diagnosis in which our age is so prolific— "We have found all the problems there are. It is now time we started to find the answers." Diagnosis without cure is a sorry prospect for any patient. Any fruitful search for a cure for the ethical maladies of this time, however, must start from the sober realization that there is no trick cure, no magic panacea, no patent nostrum, no incantation. There is no "open sesame" for all locked doors. History is strewn with futile searches for easy short-cuts, trick answers to problems as large and complex as human life itself.   Ponce de Leon's search for the fountain of youth, the perennial discovery of perpetual motion, the rigid dogmas of Marxian socialism are all examples of a credulous trust in oversimplified and premature solutions.   The teaching of Jesus' life cannot be compressed into any economic or social rule of thumb to be automatically applied and guaranteed to issue in an automatic salvation.

But in the long task, not of looking for a magic pill, but of establishing the processes leading to that abundant life which was the goal of Jesus and which alone deserves to be called social health, the record of Christianity's first facing a hostile world has for our time parallels which bring awakening rebuke and encouragement.   That little symbol of the fish worked into a mosaic in a subterranean room is a relic of another time when the mind of Jesus confronted a hostile world.   Rome, in its goals, its idols, its motives, was antagonistic to the new way of life.   Almost every point in that experience and history of the church of the catacombs brings out in shining clearness three things of primary importance for the Christianity of to-day.

That Christian company, for a time at least, escaped two dangers always lying in wait for a Christian church—the danger of a mood of defeatism and the danger of a paralyzing adaptation to its environment.   Along with these two things it preserved the positive asset of an exhilaration of spirit, an intensity of fellowship, a moral energy, which we can still feel in the New Testament like the throbbing of a great dynamo.

Defeatism and adaptation are not only lurking outside the church door.   They have come inside

and taken seats within the chancel. The mood of
defeatism is not often formally proclaimed. It is
more evident in the gently complaining mood, so
common among clergymen, the type of mentality
illustrated by General George B. McClellan in the
Civil War, who was always so painfully conscious
of the enemy's strength—real and imagined—that
he never risked a frontal engagement. It is not so
much a surrender of faith as a shrinkage of aim.
The ethical transformation of life is so large an
undertaking that it is not taken seriously. The
vigorous ardor of youth gives way to a tempered
prudence. This degeneration is pointedly satirized
by Dorothy Parker in her verses under the ironic
title "The Veteran":

> "When I was young and bold and strong,
>   Oh, right was right, and wrong was wrong!
>   My plume on high, my flag unfurled,
>   I rode away to right the world.
>
> "'Come out, you dogs, and fight!' said I,
>   And wept there was but once to die.
>
> "But I am old; and good and bad
>   Are woven in a crazy plaid.
>   I sit and say, 'The world is so;
>   And he is wise who lets it go.
>   A battle lost, a battle won—
>   The difference is small, my son.'
>
> "Inertia rides and riddles me;
>   The which is called Philosophy."

That satire does not apply to a large and vigorous
section of the church, but it is painfully true of the

attitude of many to the forthright demands of Jesus. This adaptation to environment, not in the sense of a necessary proclamation of a message in terms which can be understood, or the effective institutional expression of the message in relation to current life, but in the very different sense of the dilution and compromise of the message itself, is an ever-present danger of the Christian institution. But it is a danger unquestionably augmented by the church taking over so largely from secular education the ideal and goal of successful adaptation to environment as the end of the educational process. For the aim of a real Christianity can never be adaptation to existing conditions, no matter how snug and successful that adaptation may be, but the ethical transformation of society. It is the widespread substitution of the ideal of adaptation for that of transformation which is the source of much of the impotence of contemporary Christianity. The president of a large denominational college declared approvingly in a recent Commencement address, "Americanism is playing the game according to the rules." Exactly. "According to the rules" has been often substituted for the real object of Christianity, which is to change the rules. The words found in the hymn, "To serve the present age," have often become an unintended ironical description of wide contemporary ideals and practices. In that servitude to the present age the Christian fellowship easily becomes a chaingang in which the clanking fetters binding to the unethical motives and processes of the environment are more evident than loyalty to the timeless demands of Jesus.

It was the gradual ascendency of the mood of

political compromise which differentiated the Christian Church under Constantine from the church of the catacombs. It changed the days of grandeur into the days of bondage and dissipated the "first fine, careless rapture" of a conquering faith.

Whether Christianity can be adequate to the moral leadership of our civilization to-day and to-morrow depends on whether it can recapture that mood of its earliest days, for that is the thing so conspicuously missing over large areas of church life to-day. The churches have numbers, wealth, position, efficiency of many sorts; but anything resembling New Testament rapture, and the divine carelessness from which it came, is almost as hard to find as lost youth.

There is not much hope of recovering that mood and the power which it generated without knowing rather clearly where it came from.

One of the most striking differences between a large section of the church to-day and the Christian fellowship pictured in the New Testament is that the New Testament church was *fighting something*. All through the New Testament, particularly in the latter part of it, when the shadow of persecution and martyrdom began to fall on the little Christian group, there is an oppressive sense of a desperate conflict, a fight to the death with malignant and powerful forces of evil. One of the suggestive translations which Professor Goodspeed has made of Paul's words is, "We struggle against the ruling spirits of this dark age." The church in the New Testament never thought of itself as being in a rest camp; it was obviously on a battle line. Some of the characteristic marks of the life reflected in the New Testament are due precisely to the experience of relentless battle with the ruling and malignant forces of evil in the world. For in that life of the early church we find a buoyancy and an unhesitating faith combined to make it a tremendous moral power.

The vitality of first-century Christianity was a product and a fruit of certain attitudes and actions. It was not a thing by itself. The rapid beating of a person's heart is the result of exertion. One cannot say, "Go to now, I will have my heart beat fast." Our hearts beat fast only when we do something to make them beat fast. In a very true sense the quick beating of the heart of the New Testament church was in part a product of a life-and-death struggle with monstrous forces of evil, during which the church often looked closely into the bright face of danger.

The supreme instance of this truth is found in the book of Revelation. That book is a dark forest, but it is lighted by many bivouac fires. There can be no question but that we find in Revelation two things—first, a terrific battle with the evil order in the world roundabout, and, second, the most intense and joyful fellowship, the most heightened exhilaration, made up of faith and courage, of which literature preserves any record. It is contended here that the union of these two things is not accidental. They depend upon one another. They are always found together. If we are to recover the vitality and rapture of the New Testament experience, we must recover the New Testament fight.

The most vivid picture of this is found in the imagery of the Beast in the book of Revelation. It is a tragedy that the passages about the Beast

have been the happy hunting grounds of biblical
literalists and fanatics who have fastened the most
weird and fantastic interpretations on that much
interpreted animal.   Yet the imagery is very simple.
It was readily understood by those to whom the book
was addressed.   The Beast was Rome; it was a
succession of emperors, "a wild beast with ten horns
and seven heads rising out of the sea."

The Christian fellowship was locked in deadly conflict with the great exploiting power of its time, that
cruel, well-nigh omnipotent power which devoured
and mangled the lives of men.   The Christians were
never deluded into thinking that they could make
an easy compromise with such an evil power.   They
did not compliment it.   They heaped upon it the
ugliest and most shameful names of human speech.
They did not attempt to shake hands with it in a hail-
fellow-well-met jocular manner.   That came later in
the days of Constantine, and then the glory departed
and the church accepted the manacles of slavery.

When Christianity came up from the catacombs
to become the official religion of Rome, it left something precious down in the dark.   It gained extension; it lost its intensity.   It gained in bulk; it lost
in savor.   When it ceased being a faith of a desperate
minority and became the faith of an ever-growing
majority, it gained the whole world and lost its own
life.   Gilbert Murray says that the church of the
fourth century failed for lack of nerve.   A pregnant
saying, well worthy of pondering by the church of
any century.   From this first tragic story of Christianity's becoming a majority religion there emerged
many considerations for to-day.

The first is the necessity of seeing the clash be-

tween many of the accepted powers and motives of
our world and the purpose of Jesus. This has been
stressed in these pages with what surely has been
tiresome reiteration, but it deserves almost any
amount of emphasis for two reasons. It is at once
the condition on which every advance depends and
the one so painfully lacking among a great majority
of the churches. It is of small avail to urge, however
passionately, methods of ethical transformation upon
people who do not see with clearness that transformation is necessary. It has been said that it was
the tragedy of Francis Thompson that he never
felt at home in the world. It is our tragedy that
we do. We feel so much at home, we accept as so
inevitable and final the limits to the operation of
Christian principles that our imagination does not
grasp a world remolded nearer to Christ's desire.
That is partly because multitudes do not see Jesus.
Those are bitter and querulous words of Carlyle:
"How different is that honey-mouthed, tear-stained,
soup-kitchen Jesus Christ of our poor shovel-hatted
modern Christians from the stern-faced Christ of the
Gospels, proclaiming aloud in the market place with
such a total contempt of the respectablities: 'Woe
unto you, Scribes and Pharisees, hypocrites!' "
But the words do suggest the partial and distorted
versions of Jesus which lie at the root of much present
inertia and complacency. Jesus has become for
many an ecclesiastical figure who would be, on the
whole, rather well satisfied with our present profit
psychology. It does not flash into the mind of
multitudes that Jesus' teachings of the sacredness
of personality and the law of love are actually to be
made the ground plan of the social structure. One

of the most striking examples of that inability to conceive of Jesus in fundamental opposition to the present domination of economic gain as the chief end of man is to be found in the words of one who has acquired a wide reputation as a lay teacher in the application of Christian principles to business, Roger Babson. Writing on the topic, "What Would Jesus Do in Business?" he says:

The laws of supply and demand, of service and reward, and other economic teachings are based upon this all-pervading principle of equal reaction. The successful man recognizes this law. Jesus would be a successful business man because he would recognize the law and work in harmony with it. . . . He would recognize that the path to success, to profit, and to happiness lies in first rendering that service which will earn the reward sought.

In other words, he finds that the law of supply and demand has its source in the ethics of Jesus. That is real news. When we think of what ruthless cruelty has come from the rigid application of the law of supply and demand to labor and wages, we cannot but feel that to picture Jesus placidly accepting that law is to make a grievous caricature of him. Another part of the reason why the conflict between Jesus and many current interests is not seen more sharply is at the other end. Many do not see in clear focus the actual nature of society in which they live.

Mr. G. K. Chesterton has a striking story of a supersensitive architect and a very ugly house. This architect had been out at one time and had seen this house. It had sent him into such a paroxysm of agony that for a while his life was despaired of, and he lived in a kind of haunting fear that in an un-guarded moment he might be lured out in London for a walk and would come face to face again with that excruciatingly ugly house. So finally he hit upon a very brilliant method of avoiding that catastrophe. He felt that the only way he could be sure of never seeing the house again was to move into it and live in it. That is exactly what he did. He never saw it again and lived happily ever afterward.

That is exactly the way in which we have dealt with this world in which we live. We live in it and, therefore, we don't see it. It is only when we get a chance to look at it freshly through the eyes of Jesus, that we see the squat ugliness of many of its ruling motives. One great thing that Jesus does for a man, when he comes into a man's life as a real factor in his thinking, is to take him for a walk around the block so that he can see the house he lives in! His-torically, that is what he did for men. He took them out for a walk. He said, "Follow me." And as they responded to that invitation and walked up and down the country roads and city streets in the companionship of Jesus, they got a new look at their world.

It is through his eyes that we do get a new look at the world. Then we see that there are many things that, in our complacency, we have allowed to go into the making up of our world, which are utterly anti-Christian.

A second consideration is the necessity of avoiding the vicious separation between individual and social aspects of religion and ethics. That has torn asunder what God joined together. A pious "spirituality" which accepts the exclusion of its religion from the political and economic realm worships a God who does not really count in this world. To conceive of the gospel as concerned merely with individual salvation is to withdraw religion from the most significant areas of life, and to threaten not only the influence but the very existence of Christianity itself. Such a separation will soon make of the church a little company of people on a side street, away from the main stream of life, singing ditties about heaven. It is depressing to think of the extent to which exactly this has happened, of the measureless resources of religious emotion which might have been turned into the task of making human brotherhood a reality and which have been left to run wild in channels unproductive to the kingdom of God.

The third broad consideration is the necessity of avoiding a denaturing adaptation of the gospel to a dominant business philosophy. There is timeless truth in George Bernard Shaw's words, "The prophet is useful only so long as he is stoned as a public annoyance, calling us to repentance, disturbing our comfortable reluctance, breaking our respectable idols, shattering our sacred convictions." Set beside these noble words in inglorious contrast the words of a prominent churchman instructing canvassers for funds for building an American cathedral:

Go to the men who command great wealth either in their own right or in the trust funds which they administer. Tell them that the Cathedral and the presence of the religion which it symbolizes is the guarantee of the continuance of the social order on which their prosperity depends. Tell them that religion is the insurance of their prosperity and ask them whether they think they are paying enough for their insurance.

Such a grotesque libel on the gospel is extreme, but in milder form it has been the core of thousands of appeals for church support. The mind of Jesus is all the more an enigma to the present day because of the chanting chorus of innumerable soothsayers and smooth-sayers who intone the creed, a comfortable one to those already comfortable, that aside from a few alterations here and there, the present order of things is just about right. This has resulted in the settling down over the country of a mood of complacency which has acted like the great ice sheet which geologists tell us once settled over the northern part of North America, holding everything static and rigid. That complacency found classical expression in the Thanksgiving Day proclamation of President Coolidge in 1927, in which he declared, "Our moral and spiritual life has kept measure with our material prosperity." Witness the soothing words of Nicholas Murray Butler in a recent address, telling us that "the gain-seeking motive has lost its predominance in business" and that "public service united with just and well-earned gain has taken its place." That is a fine example of the sentimentalism which seizes on some promising evidences of a new spirit and twists them into the illusion that the whole task has been accomplished, or will soon be accomplished, by the automatic action of forces now at work. Thus the most promising movements are made to serve not as an incentive but as a sponge filled with chloroform.

CHAPTER X

OBSTACLES WITHIN THE CHURCH

To visualize the Christian task in America to-day it may help to look at it first negatively, to examine some of the obstacles to Christian transformation of society which exist in the preaching and practice of the church itself. In the Middle Ages there was drawn up a list of the Seven Deadly Sins, on which the chief weight of ecclesiastical condemnation was visited. They were: pride, envy, anger, covetousness, gluttony, lust, and sloth. Perhaps with some real pertinence a parallel list might be drawn up of the seven deadly sins of the pulpit and pew in relation particularly to the application of the gospel to society. The attempt at least may bring into a nearer range of vision some current futilities and inadequacies.

1. One of these deadly sins is *a pathetic faith in generalities*. To say this is not to deny the power of words. Words may be things. There are words, as has been truly said, which are half-battles. One of the most significant of all the titles given to Jesus is that which describes him as the Word of God. But that power of words is a very different thing from the proclamation of generalities which are hung in midair and never given a local habitation. A most dangerous delusion easily possessing the preacher is the feeling that, having talked beautifully and eloquently about a problem, he has somehow settled it. The pulpit has suffered grievously

from the sentimentalism which talks about ends
without reference to means.   Often there is in humor
a sharp expression of far-reaching incongruities of
life.   Such, at least, there seems to be in a conversation reported in the "London Opinion." An old lady
asked a bus conductor "Are you going to Dorking?"

"Yes," answered the conductor, "hurry up!"

"Oh," the old lady replied, "I don't want to go
there, but I was just thinking what a lovely day
you have got for the trip."

It is a common attitude toward the destination of
the kingdom of God on earth—"I don't want to go;
I was just thinking what a lovely trip it would be."
A Washington press correspondent has made the
claim that he could compute the longitude, latitude,
and platitude of certain senators on controversial
questions.   It is often fairly easy to compute the
latitude and platitude of certain pulpits.   It is the
platitudes unrelated to actual situations which have
a stultifying effect.   Abstract generalities have the
same relation to the cutting truths of Jesus as do
the big gilded pipes set up in front of a pipe organ
bear to the smaller ones which actually make the
music.   The imposing shiny pipes look as though
they could emit a blast which would shake a city,
but, as a matter of fact, they cannot emit anything.
They are dummies made for looks.

2. *Too little realistic thinking* is a common and
deadly sin.   The sentimentalism just referred to
results in a vicious fog of ignorance concerning the
actual results in life of forces at work in our world,
such as economic greed, the war system, and race
antagonism.   A name frequently found on Roman
Catholic churches is "The Church of the Holy Inno-

cents." This name, with a slight change in the
spelling of the word "h-o-l-y," could be transferred
to many Protestant churches—The Church of the
Wholly Innocents, for they are almost, if not quite,
"w-h-o-l-l-y" innocent of any real knowledge of the
pagan forces which block the application of their
own message. Through the reconstructed skeletons
of prehistoric animals in our museums many of us
are more familiar with the structure and nature of
beasts which millions of years ago roamed the spots
where our cities now are than we are with the beast
which roams the streets to-day. That word "beast"
as a description of exploiting greed reminds us of its
use in the book of Revelation as a symbol for Rome,
but with the difference that instead of fighting the
beast many to-day stroke it, and pet it, and say
"Nice pussy," and feel flattered when it lifts a paw
to shake hands with them in response to some
address of felicitation. Some efforts to restrain it
remind us of those relics of the genteel age of mid-
century America during which there was quite a fad
making crocheted dog muzzles.

3. *A too easy adjustment to the present order* readily
follows from these social sins. A long time ago
Ralph Waldo Emerson said keenly that the real
object of worship of many Christians of his day was
represented by the best diagonal line which could
be drawn between Abbott Lawrence and Jesus
Christ. Abbott Lawrence was probably the most
conspicuous industrial Baron of his time. He
embodied the sacred qualities of New England
shrewdness and the ability to make two dollars
grow where only one grew before. Our worship
to-day still moves along the same kind of diagonal

lines.   Some people draw their diagonal line between Napoleon and Jesus Christ, and accept the best resulting compromise that comes out.   Others favor the diagonal line which represents the compromise effected between the far more potent financial king and the Peasant of Galilee.

By this process we bleach all the color out of Jesus. Our life and words lack sting.   The anti-climax which is the inevitable doom following such diagonal manipulations is very keenly described with unconscious satire in an entry in the Journal of Samuel Pepys: "A good sermon of Mr. Gifford at our church upon 'Seek ye first the kingdom of heaven.'   A very excellent and persuasive, a good and moral sermon. He showed like a wise man that righteousness is a surer moral way of being rich than sin."   O lovely gospel!

On this entry Robert Louis Stevenson comments: "It is thus that the respectable people desire their great hearts to address them, telling in mild accents how you may make the best of both worlds and be a moral hero without courage, kindness, or troublesome reflections; and thus the gospel, cleared of Eastern metaphor, becomes a model of worldly prudence and a handy book for Pepys and the successful merchant."

To anyone interested in Christianity as a molding force in American life we cannot imagine any reading more depressing than the four chapters of the book already referred to several times, *Middletown*, which describe in a strictly objective manner the religious life of a typical American city.   The emphasis on irrelevancies, the predominance of credal orthodoxy, the setting of the seal of approval on money success, the stimulation of the profit motive, the lack of challenge to the underlying assumptions of the industrialism amid which the church has its being, the remoteness of much of the preaching, both from the deepest personal needs of individuals and the community's social needs, all picture a salt which has lost its savor and has become insipid. In these pages there is little evidence of any warm and daring human sympathy, of any insight into the complexities of the social problem or the latent tragedies of life, no emotional abandonment, no understanding of the cross, except as a decoration or a theological doctrine.

Over the spires of many New England churches there is frequently to be seen a bit of decoration which whispers perverse suggestions to the imagination. It is the weather vane. No doubt it came to be used on church spires as a protest against Catholicism and the association of the cross with the Catholic Church, and also as a piece of practical service to the community to show which way the wind was blowing. But the weather vane over the church might often take on a true and deep symbolism as the outward and physical sign of an inward and spiritual disgrace, and accommodation to prevailing winds. It pictures the frequent surrender of the moral absolutism of the cross for the pliant opportunism of the weather vane.

4. A deadly sin against the kingdom of God has been a prevalent *absorption of both pulpit and pew with problems of individual morality* while not facing the social iniquities of the time. There are many causes contributory to this individual emphasis into which we cannot enter here. It is a part of

the heritage of Puritanism discussed in Chapter III.
It is due in part to the survival of a rural culture
and social pattern which has not been adjusted to the
moral complexities of an industrial urban civilization. But it is partly due also to the fact that
violations of personal morality are both more easily
recognized, and in addition—here is the crux of the
matter—can be attacked without arousing strong
and disturbing opposition. A home-missionary
worker has given a picture of this absorption in
describing one of the feudal duchies of the coal
regions of West Virginia where the company has the
whole community clamped in the iron grip of an
economic autocracy amounting almost to peonage.
In this locality the minister of the company-con-
trolled church was conducting a fervid preaching
crusade—against Sunday baseball! In the Beards'
Rise of American Civilization there is recorded the
story of the Puritan pirate of colonial days. He
was as God-fearing a man as ever scuttled a ship.
He had gone into the business of piracy rather accidentally, having first been a privateer in one of the
frequent wars. There he found the business so
much to his liking that he kept on after peace had
been declared. One morning, while sailing the
Caribbean after a very profitable raid on a West
Indian seaport, he was horrified to discover a number
of the sailors gambling with dice on the deck of the
ship. With one leap he landed in their midst, threw
the dice overboard, and threatened to make the men
walk the plank if they did not show more respect for
God's holy Sabbath. That authenticated story
pictures the interests of Puritan pirates of the industrial age as well as of buccaneering days on the sea.

The sin is not in having an interest in personal morality, but in failing to share the love of Jesus for men. "As he saw the crowds he was moved with pity for them, for they were harassed and dejected." What words for masses of men to-day! A Christian fellowship which is not primarily moved with a pity which, like that of Jesus, dares all defiances and spares no cost, bears his name, but has not known its Lord.

5. Dare we affirm that *the present movement emphasizing worship* contains the seeds of a deadly social sin? It is hard to avoid the risks of exaggeration and misunderstanding in saying so. The development of worship, so that its re-creative force in personal and corporate life may be made available, has been so long overdue in Protestantism that now that it is here we ought to get down on our knees and thank heaven fasting. But we must watch as well as pray. The æsthetic in worship can easily be perverted into an anæsthetic for the conscience. Absorption in worship may become, and in countless instances has become, an escape from facing the ethical consequences of faith. Thus the possible dynamic may become a narcotic. The call to repentance, the sharp sting of the feeling of involvement in social guilt may be chloroformed with beauty and soft music, until the preaching of an ethical challenge laid on the conscience with clear-eyed realism and on the heart with compassion comes as an unwelcomed disturbance, just as there was an unseemly jolt in the advent of the rough, harsh-voiced Amos disturbing in Bethel the soothing ministrations of the suave and tactful priest Amaziah. The logical outcome of worship, used as a means of escape,

is pictured with unconscious irony in Bruce Barton's description of the "Church of the Future," in which the proclamation of a message is to be almost entirely abandoned in favor of worship. His picture is worth scrutinizing. It is a community church. It is, of course, an undenominational church. It is largely, if not wholly, without doctrine. It is almost without sermons. Sermons are hopelessly dull things. To use the author's own words, "On Sunday the pastor conducts three short services in the morning, beginning at six o'clock, and three in the late afternoon and evening. One may go at any time, and having bowed his head and knelt and listened to the organ and the prayers, may pass out into the sunshine and rejoice in the day. On rare occasions, such as Christmas and Easter, he preaches, and his sermons are masterpieces."

The church is also open for rest, meditation, and prayer. The pastor's main function seems to be to have his image and voice broadcast by a sort of Vitaphone to the breakfast table and to the office so that his benign figure can be seen and his voice heard as he makes what Mr. Barton calls the ideal prayer, "Prosper, I pray thee, thy servant this day." No doubt the business man will get a fine uplift from that word "prosper." The principal activity of the church is welfare work, physical, economic, mental, and spiritual.

Isn't it lovely? Such a church resembles nothing so much as a sun parlor of a country club, or the perfumed rose room of a large hotel. It is the church with the engine lifted entirely out of it. It shows a remarkable lack of penetration into the real issues of life in the world to-day, to imagine that such a

little æsthetic paradise can ever speak healingly to
the world's need and tragedy.   The gospel which is
to redeem the world must be a stout gospel.   It must
work through the lives of men and women who will
go to the cross in sacrificial warfare against the
malignant powers of evil and exploitation.

A pink-tea church will never do that.   The picture
Mr. Barton paints is just exactly the kind of church
that every reactionary and Grand Duke of special
privilege would like to see.   They do not want any
of the harsh words of Jesus against the lust of greed
which spoils and mangles life.   Handel's "Largo"
is so much more pleasant.   Many people do not want
the rebuke which the gospel of Jesus brings.   A
business-like prayer, "Prosper me to-day," is so
much more uplifting.   Perhaps it is an omission,
but if so, it is a fatal one, that nowhere in Mr. Barton's whole chapter is there any place left for the
church's touching the conscience and creating the
conviction of sin.

It is a very "pretty" religion, and that is just
what is the matter with it.   The world is not saved
by a "pretty" religion.   Jesus died on a cross, and
men who have carried his spirit into the world are
men who had a profound religion, based on the proclamation of great truths which went to the very
center of life.

6. Another form of activity which may be and
has been engaged in, with results equally vitiating
to the church addressing itself to the task of building
a more Christian order, is *absorption in its own mechanism and organization.*   That is the continual danger
of ecclesiastical organization, and as the task of ethical regeneration grows more complex outside of its

walls, the danger of occupying its attention in the
simpler and more familiar realm of its own internal
mechanism is increased.   The danger is all the more
insidious because that absorption has in itself such
large elements of real religious motive.   The institutions of religion must have vigor, its organizations
must have effectiveness, if it is to be a social force.
The danger comes when the means obscures the end,
when drilling becomes a substitute for fighting, when
the destination is forgotten in preparation for the
journey.   The busy activity of the parish routine
often becomes more frantically busy just in proportion to the loss of clearness in its grand objective.   The message which should turn the world
upside down is forgotten in the busy ups and downs
of a parochial merry-go-round.   Churches in this
predicament make the assumption that they are an
end in themselves.   As far as an observer may judge
they assume that their purpose is fulfilled if they
maintain themselves in health and prosperity,   In
this respect they are like a professional invalid
whose chief end in life is to keep himself alive.   If
he succeeds in doing this, the larger question of what
useful end his health accomplishes, is not raised.
Such churches are poor representatives of Him who
came not to be ministered unto but to minister.
They are centrifugal forces drawing inward to themselves, when they should be flinging their lives outward.

The church which makes the assumption that
maintaining itself in health and strength is fulfilling
its destiny turns the gospel entirely upside down.
The far-reaching task of the church in establishing
the kingdom of God has been well described by the

glowing words of Walter Rauschenbusch: "This high task of making human life and human society the realization of the Father's loving will for his children—this is the substance of the spiritual life, of which the services and the devotion of the church are but outward forms."

Some churches seem to assume that the world can be saved by organization. They never make that statement in so many words, but the emphasis which they lay upon organization, physical equipment, upon manipulations of one sort and another, proclaims very clearly that the church is going on the assumption that such things are of first importance.

Such churches have forgotten that the gift of organization is never ranked as of the first order in the New Testament. When the apostle Paul drew up the classic list of God's gifts to the church in the twelfth chapter of First Corinthians, the powers of organization and administration are mentioned seventh in order. The things which come first in Paul's list of gifts are those having to do essentially with the communication of life—apostles, prophets, teachers. These are supreme. When they are present, other things, such as miraculous powers, organization, supplement helpfully. But they are not indispensable. To fall into the delusion that they are of first importance is, in the literal sense of the word, insanity. It turns the whole genius of Christianity wrong end foremost.

To-day bodies of Christians are depending on organization for things it can never produce any more than an automobile engine can give birth to an orchard. One historical example of the pre-

dominant emphasis of the expansion of organization
to the minimizing of ethical challenges of the time
is to be found in the characteristic product of an
epoch of church building, the famous song of Chap-
lain, later Bishop, Charles C. McCabe, of the
Methodist Episcopal Church. All over the country
he stirred audiences by his singing his famous song,
"We're Building Two a Day." These were the
words of the first verse:

> "Extend, along the line is heard,
>   Thy walls, O Zion fair;
> And Methodism heeds the word
>   And answers everywhere.
> A new church greets the morning's flame,
>   Another evening's ray
> All hail the power of Jesus' name—
>   We're building two a day!

These lines are not mentioned for the purpose of
passing judgment on the interest in physical building
on a large scale. Into that material achievement
there went large amounts of self-sacrifice and religious idealism. The point here made is that this
era of expansiveness following the Civil War was
the era in which the country sank into the lowest
depth of political corruption which it had known
in all its history. It was an era of the scandals of the
Grant administration when morality was at a low
ebb. And in the contemporary records there is
appallingly little evidence that the church faced in
any serious way the challenge of these social im-
moralities. It was, we might say, too busy "building
two a day."

Finally, there is the exclusive sin, so general that

it seems to come under the criticism of pious generalities just mentioned, and yet it is specific enough
to warrant particular attention. That sin is the
frequent *failure to communicate an experience of God.*
It is a commonplace that the purpose of preaching
is neither discussion nor exhortation, but to bring
human lives into touch with the life of God; in
Doctor Coffin's fine phrase, "to put the hands of
men and women into the hands of God." Such an
experience brings not only individual re-creation,
but also the energizing needed for social action.
Without it the most complete program for social
betterment will lack adequate motive power. The
primary social service which the church can render
to our generation is to deepen within men the faith
that there is cosmic support for human idealism, that
the struggle for a better world is not a lonely and
quixotic enterprise, but the will of God revealed in
Jesus. The task, however, will never be accomplished, even though the ground may be cleared of
formidable obstacles. It is through positive actions
and positive convictions, through the abandon of
an exuberant faith that the impress of Jesus on the
mind of the nation must be made.

CHAPTER XI

THE LEAVEN OF THE KINGDOM

It may well seem that a good part of the scene glimpsed in these pages is calculated to induce a pessimistic mood. But even if the resulting mood verges rather nearer to pessimism than to a buoyant optimism, that in itself is a spiritual asset. No parable of Jesus has a more pertinent application to the church in the United States to-day than that of the man who waged war without having any real knowledge of the strength of the enemy. That is characteristic of so much spiritual warfare to-day. It consists in what were termed in eighteenth century military strategy, "diversions," that is, expeditions away from the main battle line. There have been a multitude of "diversions" in the history of Christianity in America, draining off energy and attention into minor and incidental engagements which had little to do with the central enterprise of establishing the kingdom of God.

The clearest sense, even an oppressive sense, of the magnitude of the task is a first condition of victory. The only hopeless state of mind is that of a deluded blindness.

Two great assets may be stressed again in conclusion. One is a fresh realization of the available resources in our national character. The other is a fresh sense of exhilaration in the task.

We have dwelt on the resources which there are

for the Christian enterprise in fundamental traits of American character. A basic Christian strategy is to restrain the forces now thwarting these traits and to release such qualities for action looking to a more ethical social order. One example of such forces needing release is the democratic spirit in American character, at present held back from finding expression in industry. Another is the spirit of independence, socially valuable, but threatened by the mass pressure of to-day. Another is the trait of adventurousness, readiness for the new, which is at present repressed in the whole realm of social and economic life, although stimulated and encouraged in mechanical and scientific realms.

From the side of the very difficulties there is a real possibility of the zest of an adventurous undertaking. In Stuart Chase's book, *Men and Machines*, the last two sentences are these: "From our brains have sprung a billion horses now running wild and almost certain sooner or later to run amuck. Where are the riders with their whirling ropes; where the light-hearted youths to mount, be thrown, and rise to mount again?" Here are the possibilities of a more daring horsemanship than ever ventured in a Wild West show. Here is the promise of a genuine thrill to take the materials which might be built into an order of comfort, well-being, and spiritual significance, and save them from being made an instrument of loot for the few and make them serve the many.

As was emphasized a few pages back, the chief among the services of the Christian Church to our generation and nation is that of bringing so vital a sense of God that it can be called an experience.

It is often in those people who are most sensitive to social wrong that this sense of God and faith in God has passed into a fog.   There have been plenty of demonstrations of the truth that a prospectus of social service can never take the place of a religion. There have also been many demonstrations of the fact that the equating of the term "God" with man's social impulses, or its use as an elusive cloud bank to describe man's social values, can never satisfy man's religious nature, or furnish the power to overcome intrenched social evils.

One of the most careful students of the machine processes in industry, R. M. Fox, in writing of the increase in the number of dramatic productions dealing with machinery, says that the worker does not want the machine in drama.   He wants relief. "He wants," says Mr. Fox, "relief in dramas which portray human personality greater than the machine."   It is a deep human want.   It is the need of the drama in the theater; it is also the abiding human need, a convincing portrayal of the worth and greatness of human personality.   The one eternal drama that does portray that is the embodiment of the love of God in Jesus Christ.   Such a need can never be met by a religion without God or one with a muffled God.   An English clergyman discovered not long ago his three children in one of their games staging a wedding.   The boy was taking the part of the minister, and the oldest girl was the bride, the younger sister the bridesmaid.   "Where is the groom?" asked the father.   "Oh," said the boy, "this is just a very quiet wedding, and there isn't any groom."   It would be a quiet wedding!   A religion without God would likewise be a very

quiet religion. It will make little disturbance in
the lives of men and bring little power to the social
tasks to be accomplished.

It should not be forgotten in connection with the
matter of keeping alive a faith in God that one of
the most effective ways of accomplishing this is not
directly persuading men to believe in God, but to
work for such a transformation of those forces in
life which now deny the value of human personality
and limit the operation of love. That will make it
more possible for men to believe in a God of love.
There is profound truth in Santayana's saying,
"Could a better system prevail in our lives, a better
order would establish itself in our thinking."

Second only to this positive need, and part of it,
is the one insistent necessity of generating in the
rank and file of the church's membership a far
stronger passion for the building of a Christlike world
and a far stronger faith in the possibility of a Christlike world ever being achieved. That is the step
upon which all waits. The declaration in the
message of the Jerusalem Missionary Conference in
1928 is a noble one, "We believe in a Christlike
world. We know of nothing better; we can be
content with nothing less." But those noble words
are an ideal rather than a description of our ruling
passion. How content multitudes of Christians are
with very much less than a Christlike world!

To bring the church to the place where that would
be a real description would be to take the longest
step toward making a Christlike world. The chief
obstacle is that we do not want it badly enough.
We do not believe in it strongly enough, we are too
easily content with less. John Ruskin once made a

memorable comment on his father—"If he would only love me less and believe in me more!" How penetrating such a judgment is! If we would only love Christ less in a sentimental, conventional way and believe in him more in the reality of our lives! What would it not mean, if as the body of Christ we would seriously say, "We will not be content under the unchallenged acceptance of any system of living and working together, which places things above men and which orders life by a passion for profit rather than service to human welfare."

The oft-repeated statement of President Charles W. Eliot of Harvard to the effect that the first requisite of a college president is a capacity to inflict pain, has an application to preaching. A prime requisite of the pulpit is a capacity to inflict pain, to induce in men and women a sharp sense of pain over the unchristian elements in their lives, pain which will awaken that moral indignation so necessary to a genuine Christianity, so woefully lacking in many churches.

Another consideration to be held in mind is a thing which has acted as a brake on thousands of efforts to create a more Christlike world. That is the fear and confusion into which Christian idealists have been thrown by the demand of privileged groups to stand and deliver their blue prints of the new Utopia. Such believers in the application of Christian ethics to industrial and political life have often shown a consternation like that of a man being held up by a thug with an automatic pistol. Not having such blue prints on their persons as were demanded, they have succumbed to a paralysis of confusion. Yet there is always an effective and adequate answer to such a demand. For one thing, the answer is that the church is not in the business of blue-printing Utopias, but is demanding a more ethical order in certain definite conditions. In the second place, Christian idealists may well say that it is not their business to work out the technical or economic specifications. There already exists enough skill and knowledge for working out a more just and ethical order. When the demand becomes strong enough, the technical knowledge will be applied to the task. The lack at present is not skill, but the demand. Such a discovery of ways and means of meeting an ethical demand has occurred again and again in the history of business. One of the most striking instances of late years is the demand by which the churches through their agencies played an effective part for the abolition of the twelve-hour day in the steel industry. "It can't be done, it can't be done," wailed the owners and directors; "you church people are a pack of muddle-headed fools for suggesting it. It shows how little you know about economics. It can't be done."

"All right," was the response, "we heard you the first time. Now do it!" They did it. There was no trouble whatever about doing it. The technical difficulties were speedily overcome when the necessity of giving up an absolute autocracy was evident from the overwhelming demand of public opinion, although in the past year it has been discovered that the United States Steel Company has gone back to the twelve-hour day in many instances.

To-day there are no inherent difficulties in humanizing labor in the machine era. There is no necessity in the processes themselves for the exploitation of men and women. Machine technique can be humanized when the demand becomes strong enough. This means the idea that workers should be treated as standardized parts in some kind of an efficiency system must be abandoned and a sound industrial psychology substituted which recognizes that men are human. The depressing ugliness of industry can be removed. Jobs can be rotated, vocational training and guidance given, and a share in the management of the plants. These would have a large effect in lifting the workers from a virtual slavery into the liberty due to human beings.

In thinking of social conditions we ought never to get away from the truth that regeneration begins with us. The possible force of the church has been disastrously dissipated by the prevalence of the feeling, "Well, this thing is so big that there is nothing that we can do about it." That is always the easy and false way out. The first demand must be on ourselves; that was part of the power of the Christian fellowship in the days of the catacombs. They were a peculiar people, marked off from others by a new way of life. We must be prepared to mark off ourselves from those who acknowledge the sway of anti-Christian motives and goals. We must be prepared to walk in a different way of life in financial, civil, home, and social relations. In other words, we are to be living protests against the present unchristian order.

Love in actual social adventure must be a part of any genuine effort to construct a Christian society. Only by actual experience can love be justified to the world as a working principle. Too often actual experiments in working toward a more ethical procedure in industry receive only the nominal interest of the churches and rarely receive any real support when those efforts are under fire. Too often there is a parallel to the action of the Oxford University authorities in regard to the new Union Building which John Ruskin was instrumental in planning and erecting. The Oxford dons agreed to have it lighted by gas, and then refused to make any appropriation for gas burners. Hearty approval for gas in principle; not the slightest provision for actually burning any! Hearty approval for Christian social principles in general; languor or frowns for even the mildest and obvious undertakings for giving the principles an actual expression. Among these social experiments which have a claim for advocacy and participation are the extension of democracy into industry in some such forms as those in which the Baltimore & Ohio Railroad shops, and the Hart, Schaffner & Marx Company, with the Amalgamated Clothing Workers have made courageous and fruitful experiments. Other means looking toward a more ethical order are the extension of the minimum wage, the extension of government ownership and control of natural resources, and the extension of taxation along lines already in operation.

Beyond such measures is the necessity of making known the mind of Christ, to the end that such knowledge will prepare the hearts and minds of men for a serious modification of our industrial system. The conditions which have engaged our attention in these pages demand more conscious functional control of natural resources and co-operative administration of industries for the purpose of meeting human needs and welfare rather than the production of large profit for the few. This does not mean that the primary reliance should be placed on legislative action. The supreme reliance of Christianity is on the multiplication of men and women who have the mind of Christ. But there must be the readiness for that Christian fellowship of life to issue in industry and business both in method and motive. Above all there must be such an opening of eyes to the working of the present motives and goals that it will be no longer possible for Christians to hold complacent illusions about them. There must be the clear-eyed recognition which Dr. Bernard I. Bell pleads for, "The church should teach that as long as any person is selfishly opposing or through indifference preventing such readjustments in our society as will remove from all men the burden and threat of poverty, he is a sinner unrepentant, a violator of the fundamental law of God."

At Christmas time, in some of our public squares in the cities, the lights of office buildings are arranged so that they shine out in the form of a cross. It is the moving symbol of the great task, the great hope of our world, that the church and the message of Jesus Christ must be in our world not merely like a little Christmas tree, a temporary addition in some city park. It is, rather, to be a part of business itself, of the things that we do for a living, and which is the texture of our daily life and the work of our whole industrial world. On that we must place the marks of the Lord Jesus. For only as we carry his spirit into the ruling forces of our work, only as we bring into business itself some of the sacrificial spirit of Jesus Christ, will we ever get on with the task and the hope of making this a Christ-like world.

It is a struggle with an aggressive foe which knows just what it wants. It is to be questioned whether history in any land has ever shown as fearless, convinced, and resourceful an economic rulership as is to be witnessed in the United States, or one which more thoroughly is set against liberalizing groups and movements. Against this the church must join hands with the American love and tradition of liberty, nurtured through three hundred years of history. What avails it if arbitrary political power was overthrown, if that power is to reappear in more oppressive form in factory and mine?

In Mr. E. C. Montague's finely written novel called *Rough Justice*, there is presented an unforgettable picture of a boy, the hero of the story, with a great power of love in him.

We see that boy taken for the first time to church, a church where his uncle was vicar. The preacher climbed the pulpit stairs and gave out a piece of terrible news—no doubt, Bron felt, because so many people were all there together and might help at once. It was a rending tale of some brave and kind man ferociously hurt a long time ago, and feeling a dreadful pain, even now, because there was something not done which he wanted them all to do for him. . . . Bron wept beside the nurse in the family pew, shrinking shamefacedly back into his corner. But the people seemed to be strangely tranquil. Instead of rushing out to help, they sang another hymn, quite slowly. Even when they came out of church they walked away as if nothing remarkable had happened and nothing had to be done. And the nurse, when questioned, only said we must not take things too much to heart—people would think us odd if we did.

"Don't take it to heart, people will think you odd." These words float in upon us through every open window. They have an unceasing pressure upon the whole population. But there sounds also another voice, a still, small voice, which says, "Do take it to heart!" For Calvary is the story of a Man who took things terribly to heart.

NOTES

PAGE

11. J. A. Spender, *The America of To-day*. Ernest Benn, Ltd., London. 1928.

15. *Christ and Human Need*. Christian Student Movement, London. 1926.

18. Sinclair Lewis, *The Man Who Knew Coolidge*. Harcourt, Brace & Company, New York. 1927.

20. Takanobu Murobuse, in New York Herald Tribune, January 12, 1920.

21. Paul Hutchinson, *The United States of Europe*. Willett, Clark & Colby, Chicago. 1929.

30. O'Higgins and Reed, *The American Mind in Action*. Harper & Brothers, 1924.

33. Phillip Guedalla, *The Second Empire*. G. P. Putnam's Sons.

39. Dean W. R. Inge, in *Science, Religion, and Reality*, by Joseph Needham. The Macmillan Company. 1928.

42. Shailer Mathews, *Jesus on Social Institutions*. The Macmillan Company. 1928.

48. Hugo Münsterberg, *American Traits*. Houghton Mifflin Company. 1901.

51. J. A. Spender, *The America of To-day*. Ernest Benn & Co., Ltd., London. 1920.

53. *America's Secret: The Cause of Her Economic Success*. By J. Ellis Barker. Published by John Murray, England.

54. T. R. Glover, *The Jesus of History*. Association Press. 1918.

60. Robert C. Binkley, "A Nation of Realtors," in The New Republic, October 9, 1929.

PAGE

60. Carl Russell Fish, *The Rise of the Common Man.* The Macmillan Company.

69. Lewis Mumford, *The Golden Day.* Horace Liveright. 1926.

79. Carl Russell Fish, *The Rise of the Common Man.* The Macmillan Company.

80. Frederick J. Turner, *The Frontier in American History.* Henry Holt and Company. 1920.

82. V. L. Parrington, *Main Currents in American Thought.* Harcourt, Brace and Company, Inc. 1926.

84. Henry Justin Smith and Lloyd Lewis, Chicago—*A Story of Its Reputation.* The Macmillan Company. 1929.

86. A. M. Schlesinger, *New Viewpoints in American History.* The Macmillan Company.

87. Stephen Leacock, *Short Circuits.* Dodd, Mead & Company.

91. Douglas Woodruff, *Plato's American Republic.* E. P. Dutton & Company.

93. Virginia Woolf, *A Room of One's Own.* Harcourt, Brace and Company, Inc. 1929.

100. Arthur Pound, "Iron Man in Industry," Little, Brown & Company. 1922.

104. Charles Morz, *The Great American Band Wagon.* The John Day Company, Inc.

105. J. A. Spender, *The America of To-day.* Ernest Benn, Ltd., London.

107. Henry N. Wieman, *Methods of Private Religious Living.* The Macmillan Company. 1929.

109. New York Herald Tribune. April 14, 1929.

109. G. N. Stevens, *The Land of the Dollar.* W. Blackwood & Sons. Edinborough, 1897.

PAGE

112. Salvadore Madriaga, in The Forum, July, 1929.

117. Robert C. Angell, *The Campus*. D. Appleton & Company. 1928.

120. Hugo Münsterberg, *The Americans*. McClure & Phillips. 1904.

120. Lewis Mumford, *The Golden Day*. Horace Liveright.

120. J. T. Adams, *Our Business Civilization*. Albert & Charles Boni. 1929.

124. John Dewey, "America by Formula," in The New Republic. September 18, 1929.

125. Robert S. and Helen Lynd, *Middletown*. Harcourt, Brace & Company, Inc. 1929.

128. New York Times, December 27, 1928.

130. George Creel, in Collier's Weekly. March 16, 1929.

134. New York Herald Tribune, January 6, 1929.

134. Willard L. Sperry, *Signs of These Times*. Doubleday, Doran and Company. 1929.

136. Durant Drake, *The New Morality*. The Macmillan Company. 1928.

137. W. A. Starrett, *Skyscrapers and the Men Who Build Them*. Charles Scribner's Sons. 1928.

141. J. A. Spender, *The America of To-day*. Ernest Benn, Ltd., London. 1929.

144. Julien Benda, *The Treason of the Intellectuals*. William Morrow and Company.

145. Stuart-Chase, *Prosperity—Fact or Myth*. Charles Boni Paper Books. 1929.

150. Reinhold Niebuhr, "We Are Driven," in Christian Century. July 29, 1929.

152. Christine Frederick, *Selling Mrs. Consumer*. The Business Bourse.

PAGE

153. Matthew Josephson, in Outlook and Independent, June 5, 1929.

157. McClure Newspaper Syndicate, December, 1929.

157. Paul M. Masuer, *American Prosperity*. Viking Press. 1929.

161. Edgar L. Bernays, *Propaganda*. Horace Liveright. 1929.

167. R. M. Frienfels, *Mysteries of the Soul*. Alfred A. Knopf. 1929.

172. Carlton J. H. Hayes, *Essays on Nationalism*. The Macmillan Company. 1926.

172. J. H. Lasswell, Northwestern Christian Advocate, February 10, 1927.

177. The Christian Advocate, November 24, 1927.

180. S. K. Ratcliffe: England Looks Toward America. Yale Review, autumn, 1929.

182. The Christian Century, February 12, 1930.

187. Dorothy Parker, *Enough Rope*. Horace Liveright. 1927.

193. Roger Babson, "What Would Jesus Do in Business?" in Christian Herald, June 8, 1929.

195. Quoted by W. Russell Bowie, in *The Inescapable Christ*. Charles Scribner's Sons. 1926.

204. Bruce Barton, *What Can a Man Believe?* The Bobbs-Merrill Company. 1927.

212. R. M. Fox, *The Driven Machine*. Leonard and Virginia Woolf, London. 1928.